MW01485602

CRUCIBLE
OF TERROR

A Story of Survival Through the Nazi Storm

CRUCIBLE
OF TERROR

A Story of Survival Through the Nazi Storm

Max Liebster

Grammaton Press
New Orleans

Grammaton Press, LLC
601 Poydras Street, Suite 2650
New Orleans, LA 70130
(504) 566-3619
books@grammatonpress.com

Permissions

The excerpts in the text of various publications and documents are found in *Viernheim zwischen Weimar und Bonn: Demokratie und Diktatur in einer deutschen Kleinstadt 1918-1949,* by Brigitte Perker, 1988, Der Magistrat der Stadt Viernheim and are quoted with permission. Following are the pages on which these excerpts appear, followed by the page numbers where they are found in *Viernheim zwischen Weimar und Bonn.*

p. 1 / p. 94
p. 3 / p. 94
p. 12 / p. 20
p. 19 / p. 156
p. 23 / p. 91
p. 29 / p. 154
p. 30 / p. 142 (school prayer)
p. 30 / p. 156
p. 31 / p. 104 ("decent Jew")
p. 31 / p. 149
p. 32 / p. 96

p. 34-35 / p. 103
p. 72 / p. 128
p. 77 / p. 129 (summer solstice)
p. 77 / p. 149
p. 136 / p. 149
p. 137 / p. 128
p. 138 / p. 155 ("Crystal Night" report)
p. 138 / p. 149
p. 139 / p. 128
p. 140 / p. 155

Crucible of Terror: A Story of Survival
Through the Nazi Storm / Max Liebster

ISBN 0-9679366-2-4

Printed in Korea

Dedication

To my father Bernhard and my mother Babette

To Willi Johe

To Ernst Wauer

To Otto Becker and Kindiger, who risked their lives

to save me from a typhus epidemic in the Small Camp

Contents

Foreword

For the first two decades of his life, Max Liebster knew the town of Auschwitz (Oswiecim) only as his father's birthplace. Liebster grew up in an observant Jewish home in a small German town, but as a teenager, he was transplanted to urban life, where his bustling routine left him oblivious to the gathering Nazi storm clouds. In late 1938, the pogrom dubbed "Crystal Night" abruptly changed things; Liebster was suddenly overtaken by the rushing tide of hatred. Young Max embarked on a nightmarish sojourn that would eventually lead him back to the place of his father's birth. In the camp at Auschwitz, Max became an eyewitness to the Nazi program of annihilation of the European Jews. Liebster survived, largely through a series of fortunate coincidences and help from unexpected quarters. Max Liebster's vivid story describes the experiences of German Jews— from initial disbelief over the virulence of Nazi antisemitism to the final agonies of the camps. Liebster's language is not designed to present a gruesome account, but his description of his experiences in five camps does nevertheless convey the terrible reality he witnessed and survived.

While he was en route to Sachsenhausen, Liebster's story departs dramatically from the familiar. By chance, he encounters an intriguing phenomenon—a group of prisoners known as the purple triangles. The purple triangle was borne by the *Bibelforscher,* or

Jehovah's Witnesses. They were prisoners of conscience, stubbornly committed to their principled nonviolence, and indomitable and brash in their condemnation of Hitler's regime. In Neuengamme, Jews and Jehovah's Witnesses are thrown together. Liebster gives us a close-up view of a victim group that seldom appears in the historiography of the Nazi era, a group that resisted Nazi indoctrination even in the concentration camps. Liebster becomes absorbed in the ideological battle he sees, for whereas the Nazis gave Jews no options for release, the Witnesses could gain their freedom, if they would just renounce their religious beliefs, something most Witnesses refused to do. Liebster, who later converted, was so profoundly affected by the purple triangles that he was moved to bear witness about their uncommon courage in the face of evil. This book is an expression of Liebster's determination to bring their little-known history to light.

In recent years scholars have focused greater attention on the non-Jewish victims of the Nazi era. A few historians have begun to fill in the historical gaps regarding the Nazi persecution of Jehovah's Witnesses. Max Liebster's memoir adds an important, humanizing chapter to a story that deserves to be known.

> — Henry Friedlander,
> Professor Emeritus of Judaic Studies
> City University of New York

Acknowledgments

I would like to thank the people and institutions who assisted me in various ways to put together my story as accurately as possible: Jürgen Hackenberger, Frau Scharf in the Reichenbach Archive, historian Hans Knapp, and the collections of the Darmstadt Municipal Archive and the Watchtower History Archive in Selters, Germany, provided historical material to confirm my memories.

Patrick Giusti provided invaluable technical help in handling the manuscript and correspondence. Monica Karlstroem translated newspaper clippings, song lyrics, and other items from the Nazi period. Elaine Siegel performed the difficult task of typing my manuscript. Eric Miller, a scholar of Jewish history, and Joseph Kempler, a survivor of Mauthausen and other camps, reviewed my manuscript and made very helpful suggestions. Charlie Miano's artistic talents resulted in a wonderful oil portrait that captures my emotions so vividly. Greg Roman created the dramatic cover design. Tobiah Waldron kindly provided my book with an index. Rick and Carolynn Crandall accomplished the editing and typesetting work despite a tight deadline.

Walter Köbe, Wolfram Slupina, and James Pellechia first urged me four years ago to undertake this writing. It proved to be a mental and emotional challenge, but I am grateful for their encouragement. Jolene Chu, who has become our "adopted" daughter, patiently analyzed my statements and skillfully refined the text so that it faithfully expresses my recollections and feelings. And I am deeply grateful to my beloved wife, Simone, who has had the challenging task over the past four years of living my memories with me and helping me to put my story on paper. Her years of devotion and support have truly been one of the most precious blessings in my life.

Stay away from Jews—and soon
we'll be rid of them, because
we don't need any Jews in Viernheim.
—*"Viernheim People's Daily," 1936*

Viernheim, Germany; November 9, 1938. The damp, gray November day had barely begun. I watched as my cousin and employer, Julius Oppenheimer, wrapped his little daughter Doris in woolen blankets and carried her out of the house. He gently laid the sleepy girl next to her mother on the rear seat of the car. Frieda cradled her daughter's head, full of curly locks, upon her shivering knees. Doris whimpered softly, her whimpers playing a duet with her mother's sighs.

Julius's brother Hugo and his young wife, Irma, climbed into the other car. Both vehicles had been hurriedly loaded with a few days' supplies and important documents.

After one last look around, we shuttered the windows and locked the doors. Julius told me to take the wheel of his shiny Citroën. In solemn procession, I followed Hugo's car out of the driveway and onto Luisenstrasse, turning right at Lorschstrasse. Around the corner in the dim light of the street lamp, one could barely make out the sign of Julius and Hugo's store, *Gebrüder*

Oppenheimer (Oppenheimer Brothers). Would we escape with our lives? Would the store and the Oppenheimer home escape harm?

The town of Viernheim receded behind us as we drove eastward toward the Odenwald Mountains. In the foothills, we passed the medieval city of Weinheim, lying in the midst of harvested grapevines. Soon we entered the barren forest. During the long drive, no one broke the silence. The serenity of the bare trees and the fresh odor of the damp earth did nothing to cut the tension. Our slow climb into the mountains belied our racing hearts— what would happen to us and to our business? Winding our way toward the misty summit, we took a secondary road that drew us farther into the forest, deeper into the gloom, and far away from any dwelling. There, far from any watching eyes, we brought our cars to a halt. For a long time we sat motionless, absorbing the deafening quiet that surrounded us.

The decision to leave everything behind had not been an easy one. When the first reports about synagogues being burned had reached us, each of us believed that such vandalism could only happen in big cities, where the culprits could hide—never in our quiet Catholic town. After all, the Nazi-orchestrated boycott of Jewish businesses in 1933 had not touched the Oppenheimers in Viernheim. Their reputation for being fair with their customers had protected them. They sold linens and fabrics to many townspeople on credit, without charging interest. The villagers far off in the Odenwald Mountains knew that merchandise purchased at Oppenheimer Brothers would be delivered to them at no extra cost.

We felt more German than Jewish. Our neighbors were good, decent folk. We trusted that they would not fall prey to the Nazi thug mentality.

Get involved with a Jew
And you'll always be cheated.
Enters the Jew and brings the devil with him!
—*"Viernheim People's Daily," 1936*

Our lives had been absorbed with making the business a success despite the hard economic times. For the past nine years, I had lived with the Oppenheimer family and had shared their joys and sorrows. During that time our hard work had paid off.

But now? Hysteria had overtaken all of Germany. Firestorms of hatred and violence toward the Jews had destroyed the memory of good deeds and burned bridges between neighbors. Nearby properties had already been set ablaze. Waves of hatred toward Jews had wrought terrible changes. Our trust in the benevolence of our neighbors had made us oblivious to the import of what was happening in the rest of Germany. But now we finally admitted to ourselves that we might be in danger.

Julius and Hugo decided we should leave while we still could. It wasn't leaving behind material things that disturbed me the most. It was the foreboding feeling that things had changed forever for us, for all Jews.

My mother was born an Oppenheimer. The archives in Reichenbach, a little town in the Lauter Valley of the Odenwald, first mention the name in 1747. A Jew bearing that name had to pay the special compulsory tax imposed on Jews. Eli Oppenheimer settled his family in the heart of this valley, tucked in the midst of the wild Odenwald Mountains in the German state of Hesse. He had chosen to leave the city for life in a primitive village.

If he had come seeking security for himself and his family, he certainly found it. By 1850, ten families bearing the name

*Synagogue de
Reichenbach*

Oppenheimer lived in Reichenbach. That gave them the number of males needed for a *minyan,* a Jewish prayer service. A small synagogue arose next to a little stream. The entire Jewish community could come to celebrate *Yom Kippur,* the Day of Atonement, and perform the ritual throwing of a stone into the water while asking *Adonai* to drown their sins. Another Oppenheimer, my grandfather, Bär, presided over Reichenbach's chorus for years until his death. He also served as cantor and as the *shohet* (a Jewish butcher who slaughters and bleeds animals in accord with the tradition—using a sharp knife and a quick stroke).

Bär lived in a tiny home not far from the synagogue. He doted on his children—Adolf, Bertha (nicknamed Babette), and Settchen. Ernest Oppenheimer, a cousin of Bär's, had emigrated to South Africa and went on to become a diamond magnate—he became Sir Ernest Oppenheimer when he was knighted in 1921. But Bär's

La maisonnette Liebster
Reichenbach im Odenwald

life of simple poverty left him neither bitter nor jealous. He delighted in friendly exchanges with all whom he met, and his warmth and vitality lived on in the minds of the villagers long after he died. When I was a boy, people would say to me, "You truly are Bär's grandson," and I glowed at the compliment.

When the time came for his daughter Babette to marry, Bär Oppenheimer received offers from the larger Jewish community in Frankfurt, where there were many more eligible bachelors. Bernhard Liebster would become Bär's new son-in-law. The devout young Jew had been born in Oswiecim (also known by the soon-to-be-notorious German name Auschwitz), which was then part of Austria. Bernhard left the big city and his homeland of Austria to move into the *shohet's* humble home in Reichenbach, Germany. He married Babette and even agreed to take care of Settchen, Babette's invalid sister. In the cramped house, he found a place to set up his cobbler's workshop. In 1908, Ida was born, followed three years later by my sister Johanna, whom we called by her nickname Hanna. Father wasn't home to witness my birth in February 1915. He was at the Russian front, fulfilling his patriotic duties and defending his adopted fatherland.

In Father's absence, Mother had to bear the load of caring for three children, as well as her frail sister. My sister Ida had to look after me. I remember that she once struggled to get me to come home. As a boy of three, I stood at the school railing, gazing at an unexpected herd that filled the school yard. So many horses! My curly, black hair and their silky manes blew as the wind carried the mingled odors of straw and horses. The World War had ended. Disillusioned, worn-out soldiers on their tired mounts returned home from east and west. Soon, for the first time, father and son would meet.

Ida took her oversight of me very seriously. One day she obtained special permission for us to go to our neighbor's home. She had to remain in the Schack's doorway while I went inside, where only males were allowed. An eight-day-old baby boy lay upon an embroidered cushion on top of a lace-covered table. Little boys stood around the table holding candles. I was given one too. The *mohel* stepped up to perform the circumcision. As soon as the baby cried out, my candle began to tremble, catching the tablecloth on fire. I collapsed to the floor. The baby's wails and the sight of blood had got the best of me—and not for the last time!

Father struggled long and hard to raise us out of dire poverty. He was a first-class cobbler, but with unemployment and inflation getting worse by the day, nobody had money for new shoes. He repaired ladies' shoes, farmers' boots, and stonemasons' clogs. He saved the leather from old

My father,
Bernhard Liebster

shoes to mend others again and again. But as time went on, fewer and fewer people were able to pay. Mother would get upset. She was the one who had to make ends meet. She noted our grocery bills in a debit book kept by our neighbor Mr. Heldmann, the kind and trusting grocer. As soon as money came in, Mum went over to the *Kolonialwarengeschäft,* a shop with all sorts of foods, to settle our debts. She grumbled constantly over our family's empty cash box.

During the deepening economic crisis, we in the rural areas could live off the land. We had a vegetable garden behind the house and a little potato field down by the plum and apple orchard. Dried apples and potatoes would carry us through the winter. During crisp autumn evenings, Dad would sit at the table after supper, peeling and slicing apples. We kids hovered nearby for samples.

Mum never stopped working. She couldn't—she had her hands full with our family of six. And her sister Settchen required extra care. Mum did all the wash by hand, using ashes instead of soap. During the summer she did the laundry outside. In the winter she washed our clothes in the kitchen, where she heated water on our little wood-burning stove. On rainy days she did the mending, somehow keeping our threadbare clothes together by patching the patches.

When the sun came out, Mum would work in the garden. She pulled weeds, sowed seeds, and cultivated the well-kept rows of vegetables. Our little plum orchard yielded baskets of ripe fruit. Mum removed the pits and brought the fruit to our neighbor's house, where there was a large built-in basin in the cellar for making jam. Mum had to stir and stir and stir to keep the mixture from burning. The exquisite aroma of her frothy jam swirled up from the simmering copper vat and wafted across the street to the school yard, summoning me home during recess for a slice of bread and sweet foam. The jars of jam would last us the entire year.

My school in Reichenbach

Day after day Mum hovered over the hot stove. Our meals, though very simple, were delicious. She would buy grease from the kosher butcher with which to make gravy, the sole embellishment for our dinner of potatoes. And how she worked to keep the dairy utensils separate from the meat ones! Faithfulness to Jewish tradition meant that the two sets were stored in two different cabinets and had to be washed separately as well. No wonder I hardly ever saw Mother sit down!

Sometimes when Aunt Settchen was not lying under a heavy down-filled comforter, she would sit in her armchair wrapped in layers of blankets. Only her dark, cavernous eyes showed. Or she would stretch out her long, bony fingers, asking for a cup of herb tea to help her digestion. She anxiously awaited her small pension. On the 10th of each month, she would say, "In five days it will be the 15th; half of the month is gone. Then, only two more weeks

My school picture (third row, second from left)

until my payment comes!" She would sit and look out the window next to her chair. Her dark eyes would suddenly light up when she spotted Julius and Hugo, her cousins, coming up the street. They never failed to stop by when they did business in the nearby villages and farms. They always had kind words, smiles, and a little cash for Aunt Settchen.

Ida hated school, but she wasn't afraid of hard work. In 1924, at age 16, Ida finished school and looked for a job as a housekeeper. She wanted her independence as soon as possible. I was nearly ten years old by then and glad to be out from under her diligent mothering. We never played together anymore. I had my

From left to right, our three neighbors, me, Mother and Father at the Felsenmeer

own friends. Together with the boys, I slid on my feet along snowy Binn Street or down the frozen Lauter River, ran about green meadows, shuffled through drifts of crisp leaves, watched the neighbors' goats, and played with a boomerang. A brief moment of inattention and I was marked for life when the boomerang swung around and hit me square on the chin.

The Felsenmeer—the sea of stones—was my favorite playground. Sometimes my family would take our Sabbath walk here. It was right at our doorstep and within the limit of a Sabbath day's journey.

Cascades of sleek boulders seemed to tumble down from the Felsberg summit, which culminated at 514 meters and ended in the meadow. Legend has it that a giant living in the Hohenstein Mountain had a serious quarrel with the Felsberg giant. The Hohenstein giant hurled the mammoth stones across the valley.

The Felsberg giant was buried by the stones and imprisoned in a terrifying abyss. Climbers who stepped too heavily on those rocks might hear him roar!

As my friends and I ran down the path alongside the Felsenmeer, our boyish laughter echoed loud and clear throughout the majestic forest. If we stood quietly, we thought we could hear grumbling noises from under the rocks. Sometimes we glimpsed the giant's eye, twinkling blue or dark gray, depending on the color of the sky. The eye peered out from the bottom of the stony river, which gave us crystal-clear water to quench our thirst. We cooled our red faces and splashed one another. The spring is still called Friedrichsbrunen, named after a German legend of ancient times.

The haunting legacy of the gray granite boulders had spooked people since time immemorial. During heathen times, on nights of the full moon, cloaked figures at secret meetings pronounced terrifying spells and sacred vows, summoning spirits to rise up from the abyss. But for my friends and me, the forest with its bewitching stony river held no secrets anymore. We jumped from one monster to another, competing to be the first to reach the Riesensäule. This giant column, a fallen pillar, was more than nine meters long and four meters around. Hewn from a single piece of bluish granite, the masterpiece had been erected about 250 C.E. by the Romans. It had a 60-centimeter-high niche to house an idol. The Riesensäule pillar survived the Roman departure and continued to be used as a holy site by an ancient Germanic tribe that held sacred dances around the stone in springtime. It later became a Christian shrine devoted to Saint Boniface. The sacred fertility dances continued for more than ten centuries, alongside Catholic rites. In the middle of the 17th century, a Catholic priest by the name of Theodore Fuchs converted to Protestantism. He established himself as a minister in Reichenbach (1630–1645) and pronounced a prohibition on the heathen dances. When his proclamation proved to be of no avail, he took the drastic measure of toppling the pillar.

As children, we were far removed from the worries of the postwar generation. We heard adults speak often about the World War and the hated French occupation of the Ruhr, the land of iron mines. Or they talked of inflation, lamenting the ever-rising price of groceries and the diminishing

At the Riesensäule in 2000

value of the mark. What cost 40 marks to buy in 1920 when I was five, cost 77 marks a year later, and 493 marks a year after that. As bad as those increases were—prices doubling and tripling each year—in 1923 inflation went wild. In January of 1923, that same 40-mark item would have cost 17,972 marks; by July, 353,412 marks; by August, 4,620,455 marks; by September, nearly 99 million marks; by October, 25 billion marks; and by November, more than 4 trillion marks. People needed a wheelbarrow full of money— 21 billion marks—to buy one loaf of bread! I only knew that Father gave me 10,000-mark notes to play with.

The grown-ups often discussed politics—Socialists, Communists, Worker Party, Zentrum Party—all words with no meaning to us young ones. One thing we did know: People were out of work, including some of our fathers and older brothers. Some, it was said, had to stand in long soup lines. There were rumors of unrest in the cities.

Things were no better in the Lauter Valley. The two small factories, a paper mill and a manufacturer of prussic acid, had only a handful of orders to fill. Even the main industry of the valley—stonecutting—had dropped off considerably. There was little demand for cut and polished red, gray, or blue granite for monuments, buildings, and gravestones. For the young children of the common people, the prospect of work was nonexistent.

My mother's cousins Julius and Hugo proposed to my parents that when I finished school, I could stay with them and their elderly mother in Viernheim. They could use my help in the Oppenheimer Brothers store. They would also send me to a business school nearby to receive training as a salesman. This offer provided some peace of mind for my family.

By now, Ida worked as a maid, and Hanna, my quiet and studious sister, was being trained as a secretary at the paper mill.

As for me, I was about to become a man—the time had arrived for my Bar Mitzvah. In preparation for the big event, I went to the town of Bensheim every Sunday. Our rabbi lived here, at the entrance of the Lauter Valley. On foot or by bicycle, I savored the seven-kilometer trip through lush meadows. I was the only candidate from the valley preparing for the Bar Mitzvah reading of the Torah. The rabbi, an open-minded and respected man of great patience, helped me with the pronunciation of the text. I struggled with the strange Hebrew characters, and it was even harder to remember what they stood for. Understanding is not the important thing, I was told, but rather the exact pronunciation of the Hebrew text in the sacred language of God. By the time I was 13, my reading was going smoothly. I eagerly awaited the day when my boyhood would end and I would be counted as a man. Then I could be included in a *minyan,* a group of ten adult male Jews, who had to be present to hold a public Jewish prayer service, such as *Kaddish,* a special prayer that the bereaved recite for the dead.

The big day arrived. I felt nervous and excited at the same time. The rabbi came to our little synagogue. He gave a heartfelt welcome, stepped down from the platform, and sat among the men in the audience. My mother and sisters sat in the balcony, the place for the women. My heart pounded as I climbed the two steps and opened the little door of the engraved wooden barrier separating the Jewish congregation from the platform. Here in this special place, the holy writings were usually kept in a sculpted wooden closet, hidden from the view of the audience by a burgundy curtain. Awaiting me on a pulpit in the middle of the stage lay the Torah scroll, unrolled to reveal the portion of Scripture I would read. The holy scroll was bathed in the light of a candelabra with seven branches.

For days I had been dreading the sacred reading. Now my stomach was in knots, and my mouth felt like cotton. Behind me, I could feel the presence of the whole community. Like me, they either wore hats or *yarmulkes,* and some bore on their shoulders the *Tallith,* a blue-and-white-striped prayer shawl with silver seams and fringes. Some men would take the fringes, touch their personal prayer books, and kiss them each time God's holy name appeared in the text. I learned that as sinful men, we should not pronounce the most sacred name, written in the four Hebrew letters called the Tetragrammaton. It had to be replaced by *Adonai,* which means "Lord," or by *Adoshem,* which means the "Lord of the Name." *Never* should the holy name cross our sinful lips. I used a silver pointer to trace the words from right to left upon the scroll. My reading became confident and fluent. I stepped down

Leopold and Nathan Liebster

to be congratulated by all. I was now a man.

After the ceremony, the rabbi came to our home. As was traditional, we should have had a feast in honor of our special guest and to commemorate my Bar Mitzvah. Instead, the meal was very plain, and the guest list small. Father's younger brother, Nathan Liebster, a cobbler like him, lived in Aschaffenburg. Nathan and his family were the only ones present for our celebration. Mother's brother, Adolf Oppenheimer, couldn't come. He lived in Heilbronn and had a hard time doing the daily chores in his men's clothing shop. He was sickly; he just could not afford to make the trip. Father's third brother, Leopold Liebster, a tailor who lived in faraway Stuttgart, had not been invited at all. More than distance separated my father and my uncle. Leopold had married out of our faith. His Catholic wife refused to have her children raised in the Jewish religion. Leopold did not want his children to become Catholics, so they raised the children as Protestants.

My Bar Mitzvah pleased my father, who was a devout man of prayer. My bed stood in the corner of his workshop, among piles of leather skins and shoes. From there, in the early mornings, I watched my father say his prayers. He stood at the foot of his bed, the prayer shawl upon his shoulders, the prayer book in hand, and the *Tefillin* (passages from the Torah written on parchment and placed in leather coverings) wrapped around his left arm and hand. Leather straps held the little Scripture case that hung on his forehead between his eyes. He chanted parts of the prayer while rocking back and forth. Each time he took the prayer shawl from his shoulder to pull it over his head, I knew that he had encountered God's holy name. Before Dad started his day, he would *daven* (pray) for one hour. Even when he had to leave for the city at 4:00 a.m., he never failed to rise an hour earlier to say his prayers.

I would have loved to become a *hazzan* (cantor) like Grandfather. The villagers always told me that I was the exact image of Grandfather Bär Oppenheimer.

Though I looked like my grandfather, we differed in one respect. I had always been weak around blood. I remembered when I had fainted at the baby's circumcision so many years ago. My parents may have hoped that I would follow in Grandfather Bär's footsteps and become a *shohet*, but I was not suited for it. I happened to be at the kosher butcher's one day when a cow was brought in for slaughtering. Several men surrounded the pitiable animal. They tied its legs together and flipped the animal onto its back. They held the cow's head firmly so that it could not move. Then the *shohet* wielded his razor-sharp knife with a single stroke. In a split second, blood spurted from the cow's throat. After the animal was bled, the *shohet* examined the contents of its stomach and looked at the liver to determine if something the cow had eaten, such as a nail, might have rendered the meat unclean. If nothing in its entrails had defiled the cow, the butchering could begin. Tradition or no tradition, the bloody sight left me feeling sick.

The year of my Bar Mitzvah, Hanna, my beautiful 17-year-old sister, finished her secretarial training at the paper mill. She had black velvet eyes and wavy ebony hair, along with intelligence, determination, and good work habits. Her employer asked her to

From left to right, Ida, Father, Hanna, me,
Mother and Aunt Settchen (seated)

stay on at the mill, to the great relief of my parents. Our financial crisis deepened as Father's clients took longer and longer to pay off the credit my father patiently extended. The Jewish communities knew about our dire situation. They thought of Father whenever they needed a man for the *Kaddish minyan* and would be very generous in covering his travel expenses. If the funeral was in a large city, Father would spend all the money he received on leather skins, much to Mother's disappointment.

When I finished school in 1929, my parents decided to accept the offer from Mother's cousins, the Oppenheimers, to give me a job in their store. Since I was determined to work hard and to be self-supporting, I bade farewell to my family and to my carefree childhood days. I was a penniless, 14-year-old country boy setting off for a free education and a new opportunity in the big town of Viernheim. The Oppenheimers would give me room and board in exchange for the housework I would do for Hugo and Julius's elderly mother. I would also have to take care of my own little room in the Oppenheimers' attic. A whole room for myself! At home I only had a bed of my own.

I didn't realize how difficult it would be for me to trade the Lauter Valley for Viernheim. Viernheim, with its 20,000 inhabitants, was only 25 kilometers away from home. But it might as well have been on a different continent.

Viernheim was situated in a wide open land where thriving asparagus and tobacco fields sprawled under an endless sky. For centuries the fertile flood plain of the Rhine River had nourished the soil and brought prosperity to the region. Without the protection of the mountains, the land lay exposed to the four winds. I felt vulnerable in the windy flatland.

Viernheim supplied laborers for the Mercedes-Benz plant and other factories in the nearby industrial cities of Ludwigshafen and Mannheim. Thus, the population was a mix of factory workers and farmers. In the center of town were the City Hall, the Catholic church, assorted small shops, and *Gebrüder Oppenheimer,* with its four display windows. The well-kept homes of the rich clustered tightly around the Catholic church. A little farther away was the business school and, a few blocks behind that, the synagogue.

Our work schedule started at dawn and finished long after the store closed. Early in the morning before opening time, I had to clean the store. New merchandise had to be unpacked and the shelves stocked. Then once a week, all four shop windows had to be washed, and I had to redo the window display using no money but all my ingenuity. All day long, all week long, I climbed up and down the ladder to get items for the customers, straightened the piles of goods, waited on Julius, Hugo, and their mother, and even worked on the cars. And there was still more to do. The Oppenheimers had out-of-town customers to whom I brought samples and deliveries. My employers trusted me to drive the Citroën, even though I was only 16. Despite the extra cushion on the seat, I could hardly see over the dashboard, and to other drivers and pedestrians, it looked as if the car had no driver. I would chuckle when people panicked, thinking they were seeing a runaway car.

> Shop signs saying "German store"
> are a true blessing. . . .
> Here [a German man] can be sure that
> he has not given his
> hard-earned savings to the
> enemy of all that is German, the Jew. . . .
> A true German will shop only in German stores!
> —*"Viernheim People's Daily," December 10, 1934*

Most of the townspeople received their pay on Saturday. So they would often ask us to come by on Sunday to pick up a small payment toward their bill. The Oppenheimers extended credit without charging interest, but a few customers even exploited that generous arrangement by not paying their bills at all. Bookkeeping kept us busy in the evenings and on Sundays. I took pride in my work, even in little jobs like winding up the smallest bits of string, flattening boxes, and folding wrapping paper. The two brothers ran an efficient and orderly business, and they appreciated my diligence.

Life with the Oppenheimers also introduced me to an entirely different way of Jewish life. There was hardly any evidence in the Oppenheimer home that its occupants were Jewish. To my surprise their mother did not light the two Sabbath candles on Friday evening, nor did pictures of Moses or Aaron hang on the wall. They didn't have two sets of dishes—one for meat and one for dairy. Back at home, when a kitchen knife belonging to the meat set came in contact with dairy products, Father buried the defiled blade in the ground for seven days to purify it. The Oppenheimers may have eaten kosher food at home, but when we drove through the Odenwald Mountains, we would sometimes eat in restaurants where the smell of smoked ham was unmistakable and the patrons dined on platters of meat drenched in milk gravy.

The Oppenheimer store even stayed open on the Sabbath. After all, Saturday was payday—the best day for business. Besides, like every other business in town, the store had to close for all the Catholic holidays. How could they also afford to close for Jewish holidays like *Rosh-Hashanah* (the Jewish New Year) as well? Of course, they observed *Yom Kippur* (the Day of Atonement). But what a difference from the way we had celebrated it at home!

At my boyhood home, on this most holy of days, my family would fast from evening to evening and attend the special synagogue services, including the *Kol Nidrei,* the haunting melodic prayer annulling any rash vows made during the past year. Before asking forgiveness from God, we would ask forgiveness from one another. My family made extensive preparations before *Yom Kippur.* Father took a chicken by its legs, its wings beating the air. He swung it over his head and mine (since I was the only male child) and spoke some Hebrew words. Then he turned the bird over for the ritual slaughter. *Yom Kippur* begins in the evening. We all took a complete bath, which was quite an ordeal because we had to heat the water on the stove. Only then would we attend synagogue.

A few days after *Yom Kippur* comes the festival of *Succoth,* or booths. We would sit together in a booth that Father had erected in our garden. There we prayed and took our meals. In the evenings we could see the stars through the leafy branches overlaying the top of the booth. Grapes and fruit adorned its walls, an expression of thanksgiving for the year's harvest. The frail covering of the booth reminded us of the tents in which our ancestors dwelt in the Sinai desert.

At the Oppenheimers' there were no booths, no thanksgiving prayers, only business. *Succoth* was seldom mentioned, and *Hanukkah* never. Unlike some Jewish families in Viernheim who burned candles at their windows, the Oppenheimers' windows remained dark.

I had at least expected to take part in the cleansing ritual for *Pesach,* the Passover, packing and carrying away all the *khometz* kitchenware—dishes, forks, and spoons that had had any contact with leaven. When I lived with my family, I used to heat the stove until it glowed red and chase after the smallest crumb of leavened bread. Only then could we bring the special *Pesach* utensils into the kitchen to be used during the week of unleavened bread. But the Oppenheimers never ritually cleansed their kitchen.

I missed my family and the festive *Pesach* atmosphere, with the decorated table glowing in the light of the menorah. But even more, I missed the *seder,* the Passover meal. Each of us would be seated at the table with his own *Hagadah,* the special Passover prayer book. Being the youngest male, I would ask the Four Questions, starting with, "What makes this night different from all other nights?" Father chanted the story from the *Hagadah,* explaining the liberation from bondage in Egypt. Upon the table were the *Haroseth* symbols: grated apples with cinnamon, its brownish color representing the clay the Israelites used to make their bricks, and ground horseradish, which made us all shed tears.

Next to the table, Mother prepared the *seder* bed. She spread a fine linen cover over the couch and placed a silk pillow at the head. We wrapped up some matzoh and filled a glass with red wine, just in case the Messiah arrived and wanted to partake of the meal. We left the wine and matzoh out during the whole week of unleavened bread. Thereafter, the matzoh would end up behind the picture of Moses. As a little boy, I would reach behind the picture and secretly nibble on the Messiah's meal.

Unlike my parents, the Oppenheimers gave no thought to the coming of the Messiah. Their empty *Pesach* consisted only of unleavened bread and a token appearance at the synagogue. Even at *Pesach* the business had first place. Hugo and Julius claimed that honesty and hard work were worth just as much as the observance of religious tradition. By their fairness, they helped people weather the economic depression—surely this was a *mitzvah,* a good deed. As time passed, I began to share their zeal for the business.

In 1929 just when I started to attend business school, the economy showed some signs of revival. It proved to be an illusion. The tidal wave that started with the crash on Wall Street swept mercilessly over Germany, plunging people into desperation. Julius even complained that I had become too expensive for them. The unemployed lined up restlessly each day to get their work certificates stamped so that they would be counted as needy.

Taken at business school

By the time I finished my three years of schooling, the air was tense with fear and frustration. I could see it in our customers. In the streets, marching hordes followed behind their party flags shouting slogans. The workers and unemployed together vented their anger. When factions clashed, it was wise to get out of the way. Riots flared up all over the land.

It seemed ironic to me to see the very same people who clashed in the streets come together on Catholic holidays. They walked behind a cross held aloft by the priest. Arrayed in ceremonial garments, he led the procession out of town and into the fields, where he bestowed his blessing. The sight of carved images evoked in me a deep-seated repugnance. The Torah stated clearly: "You must not make for yourselves a carved image." Truly I dwelt in an alien land!

> On Easter night Catholic youth would set fire to
> a pile of wood on the church square, and
> after receiving the priest's blessing
> and being sprinkled with holy water,
> they proceeded to march up to Jewish properties
> with burning torches, yelling: "The Jew is dead!"
> —*Recollections of Viernheim resident*
> *Alfred Kaufmann*

To my great surprise, when I graduated from business school, the Oppenheimers asked me to stay on as an employee—quite a respectable opportunity for a 17-year-old. It did not take long for the customers to ask to be served by "Mäx'che."

Work hours never seemed to end; by evening I was worn out. I rarely had time for myself. I seldom managed to attend balls held by the Jewish community in Mannheim—not to mention the occasional ones in Viernheim, where more than 100 Jews lived. The non-Jewish dances on Saturday evenings were more convenient.

They were my sole entertainment. Music inspired me, vibrating the fibers of my being, especially when I held in my arms a girl who knew how to waltz. I attended a few dances, even though most of the girls wouldn't dance with me. I managed to find an exceptionally tolerant Christian girl, and she was a good dancer too. Ruth, a vivacious young lady, wasn't ashamed to dance with a Jewish boy. I felt as if I were in heaven when we waltzed. But the music also made me melancholy. It brought back my dream of becoming a cantor like Grandpa Oppenheimer.

Julius and Hugo had no time for music, and I too had become completely absorbed in the business. The time came when the two bachelors would make a choice among potential brides. According to their criteria, the girls had to be Jewish and had to come with a solid dowry, which they thought necessary for a prosperous life. To me, the whole affair seemed more like negotiations over the purchase of a set of furniture than the choice of a companion for life. Hugo and Julius discussed the terms of the marriage agreement with their mother, who rendered her opinion. She lived just long enough to see her sons married—Julius to Frieda, and Hugo to Irma. Julius and Frieda's firstborn, Doris, came along as a true consolation after the death of her grandmother. I became Doris's favorite uncle.

Frieda Oppenheimer
(Darmstadt State Archives)

Julius Oppenheimer
(Darmstadt State Archives)

Irma Oppenheimer
(Darmstadt State Archives)

Hugo Oppenheimer
(Darmstadt State Archives)

2

The November day of our escape seemed endless. A heavy fog rose from the valley and intercepted the pale autumn sun. About seven or eight years old, Doris was too young to know that we had fled for our lives, but she sensed our anxiety and was restless and cranky. The dampness, the drafty cars, and the tension chilled us to the bone. I didn't know why—perhaps it was a combination of anxiety and cold—but Julius and Hugo took turns getting out of the cars, stamping their feet in the cold like nervous horses. By nightfall we had another decision to make. It was impossible to stay overnight in the woods where we had parked—hunters might come around early in the morning. Besides, the cars wouldn't protect us from the cold. This place in the forest had proved to be a good hiding place during daylight hours, but what now?

We decided to drive to an isolated inn situated in the remotest part of the Odenwald Mountains, a place where no one would know us. The fog dampened our headlights and the sound of the motors, making our trip through the mountains less conspicuous. The anxiety we felt in the forest intensified as we neared the place we hoped to stay overnight: Would this decision prove to be our undoing? We viewed ourselves as German. The Oppenheimers were wholly assimilated; only their surname identified them as being Jewish. My surname, Liebster, is German and means "most beloved." Even in Viernheim the Oppenheimers had been discreet—not even a menorah in their apartment window to give them away. But now we felt in danger of betrayal. Our papers branded us "Israel" or "Sarah," names forced upon us, and all Jews, by the Nazi officials.

That night at the inn, I was haunted by visions of the fearsome plague of Nazism spreading across the country. People had changed so suddenly. The lines between friend and enemy had blurred. I felt like the solitary prey stalked by a beast I neither knew nor understood.

It was in January 1933 that President von Hindenburg had unexpectedly appointed a reichschancellor named Adolf Hitler. I was just 18 years old at the time, and I heard some of our customers denounce this event as a dangerous move. Soon, however, their voices fell silent. Nazi Brownshirts* rounded up political opponents, confiscating their papers and books and breaking up their meetings. Suddenly, there were no more rowdy marches and clashes in the streets. Public places were once again safe; children could return to playing outside. Now one party, the Nazi Party (the NSDAP),** controlled the country. Germany had become a police state, but the populace welcomed the new calm, which in the minds of many made up for the fact that some experienced a loss of liberty. In any case, people dared not express their innermost feelings. The threat of being hauled away as a dissident left

---

* The Sturmabteilung (SA), also known as Brownshirts, were used by Hitler to gain political power through the use of street violence and the intimidation of political opponents.

** *Nationalsozialistische Deutsche Arbeitspartei,* or National Socialist German Workers Party.

most citizens numb with fear, ready to conform to the growing pressure.

JUDA VERRECKE!
(Death to Judaism!)
—Nazi slogan painted on walls and windows

From the beginning of his political career, Hitler furiously denounced the "worst" enemies of the State—the Communists and the Jews. Hitler's message was intensified by propaganda minister Joseph Goebbels. In his hysterical talks, Hitler promised employment, a Volkswagen, and better housing for the common people, the *Volk*. Factories had to come to a standstill while the workers listened to Hitler's ranting lectures. Indeed, the Führer did provide jobs. Every morning all sorts of men cycled past our store with shovels tied to their bikes. Instead of standing in soup lines, they had work—maybe not the type they would have chosen, but at least they earned their bread. Hot or cold, fog or rain, they labored to level the ground along the Rhine River for the future autobahn, Germany's first highway.

The Jew greedily stretched out his claw in order to pull the
German farmer into the abyss; that is when Adolf Hitler came
and stopped them—and Germany was released!
—German Farmers' Special Day

The farmers fell in step with the new regime, and this helped the economy. The government moved to protect farmers' property from lenders—if the farmers could prove that they were of pure "Aryan" stock. The masses hailed the quick economic recovery and seemed blind to the gradual strangulation of freedom. They hailed Hitler as their savior.

Adolf Hitler, you are our great Führer.
Thy name makes the enemy tremble.
Thy Third Reich comes,
Thy will alone is law upon the earth.
Let us hear daily thy voice
and order us by thy leadership,
for we will obey to the end and even with our lives.
We praise thee! Heil Hitler!

—*School Prayer*

We began to hear people make statements like, "Hitler wants order and decency. Germany should rally around its leader." The *Heil Hitler* salute replaced the common greeting. It served as a constant reminder that *Heil*—salvation—comes through the Führer. It seemed that everyone went along, whether they wanted to or not. Who would dare refuse in public? Any possible voice of dissent had been terrorized into silence by the threat of "protective custody" in a concentration camp. I could see that our own customers voluntarily shut their ears to grim rumors of atrocities that were now beginning to circulate.

Viernheim stands loyally by Adolf Hitler and the Fatherland!
. . . Viernheim is Germany—and we are a great people—
in one beautiful national community!
Germany above all—and our Führer Adolf Hitler above all!
Hail Germany—Hail the Führer!

—*"Viernheim People's Daily," March 30, 1936*

The combination of guaranteed work, a low crime rate, and plenty of food acted like a sedative. Few raised a word of complaint against the degrading posters that depicted the Jews as an evil presence. Law after law hemmed in our freedom. The government organized boycotts against Jewish businesses. Julius and Hugo's brother, Leo, had been forced to sell his candy distributorship for almost nothing to an "Aryan." He then had to go to work in a factory. But because of their good relationship with their customers, Julius and Hugo felt safe, despite the fate of their brother, Leo.

> It is an outright contradictory statement to say: "A decent
> Jew," since the expressions "decency" and "Jews" are
> contrary terms, excluding one another.
>
> —*"Viernheim People's Daily," 1938*

Newspaper articles told ugly tales about Jews. Signs appeared forbidding Jews to go to public places such as theaters or parks. Because of their inferior "blood," Jews could not be civil servants or teachers. Antisemitism even grew among educated Germans, who rushed to fill vacancies created by the ouster of Jewish academics and professionals.

Frenzied youth raised their arms and voices to hail the Führer, not of Germany alone but of the Third Reich.*

> Our banner flutters before us.
> Into the future we'll pull man for man.
> We march for Hitler through night and through hardship
> With the flag of youth for freedom and sustenance.
>
> —*"Hitler Youth Banner Song"*

As I witnessed the Hitler Youth parades, my blood turned to ice. I beheld the heaving sea of swastika flags. I saw the edge of the abyss. German veterans sought to shed the humiliation of the World

---

* The Nazi regime used the term "Third Reich" to refer to Germany and its territories. This term also had strong historical associations with the Holy Roman Empire (First Reich) and the Bismarck era (Second Reich) and a religious association with millennialist Christian views. Reich means "kingdom."

War and greeted the resurrection of the German military with great satisfaction. Hitler's success in Austria and the Munich accord with Daladier of France and Chamberlain of Britain had elevated Germany's international status. The *Volksgemeinschaft** seethed with fanatic pride.

> The population demands that all who
> do business with the Jews
> be excluded from any benefits provided by the Reich…
> —*"Viernheim Gazette"*

Jews were now making desperate plans to escape. My sweet sister Hanna had worked loyally and efficiently for almost ten years as a secretary at Tempels' paper mill. But Nazi pressure on the management resulted in Hanna's dismissal. An "Aryan" took her job. Shortly before the November 1938 pogrom, some emigration facilities were operating. Hanna made a quick and courageous decision. A Jewish organization was sending young married couples to Argentina, where land and livestock could be obtained on credit. Adolf Strass, the son of a Jewish wine-maker from Rhine Hessen, asked her to marry him so they could qualify for the farmland in Argentina. Hanna accepted the uncertain offer in order to escape the new Dark Ages and in the hopes of being able to rescue her family. She married the stranger in Reichenbach in February 1938. I briefly met Adolf the day of their wedding, a very sad occasion. There were no vows of love and devotion exchanged, no festive ceremony. Adolf came just long enough to sign the papers and then left again to prepare for their emigration. My sister was to follow him to Mainz a few weeks later.

---

*This Nazi term is a combination of the word *"Volk,"* literally meaning "nation," and *Gemeinschaft,* or "community." According to Nazi usage, *Volk* became associated with notions of "Aryan" racial unity, purity, and superiority. A pure-blooded master race was to be the common goal. Each member of the *Volksgemeinschaft* had an equal and solemn responsibility to defend the oneness and greatness of the German nation.

Ida, my older sister, lost her job as a maid. The family she worked for suddenly realized that she was Jewish, a racially inferior woman. This pure "Aryan" family could no longer tolerate her presence. They literally chased her out. Determined to emigrate to Palestine, she joined a Zionist organization and trained to take up life on a kibbutz. The waiting list was very long. While she waited for word, she met Sydney Nussbaum, a young man who had been sent to Buchenwald concentration camp after the pogrom in Hamburg in spite of the sacrifice his family had made for Germany. Sydney's father and his four brothers had all been killed in combat in the World War. While in camp Sydney had received his immigration papers from the U.S., which allowed him to walk out, empty-handed but free.

Sydney related frightening stories about his time in Buchenwald. He had seen an old Jewish man in the camp meet a violent end at the hands of a sadist. Sydney himself had undergone drastic weight loss in just a few weeks, which left him terribly weakened. But he had made it out of camp alive—so many others had returned to their families in black boxes.

Sydney was headed for West Virginia to work at Sloan's, a Jewish-owned department store. He wanted to rescue Ida and asked her to marry him. He promised that when he got to Sloan's, he would ask for the needed papers to bring his wife over.

Despite the oppressive mood, there were some bright moments. I had met a charming young lady of 20, Laure Eckstein. Laure and I tried to dance away our fears together at the Jewish balls in Mannheim. She worked at Rothchild's store in nearby Weinheim with Fanny Oppenheimer, the sister of Julius and Hugo. I introduced her to my parents. Her bubbly and outgoing nature ignited a flame in my heart. I lived for the days that I would be sent to decorate the window display at Rothchild's. I was 24, and had it not been for the uncertainty of the times, I might have married her. But when things began to look threatening, Laure's father decided to leave the area.

We had fled Viernheim reluctantly, believing deep down it was unthinkable that our customers would yield to antisemitism. After a few days in hiding, Julius and Hugo convinced themselves that the danger had passed, and they decided to return to their home and business. All the same, we felt nervous as we drove back into town. As we rounded the corner and pulled up to the Oppenheimer Brothers store, we were shocked at the sight of broken glass and shutters torn from their hinges. We stood numbly on the sidewalk and stared at the desolation. Every stick of furniture had been smashed, and all the shelves were stripped bare—a testament to the fury of Nazi vandals.

With bitterness we had to face the painful reality—our naivete had been ravaged by Germany's antisemitic storm. The mayor came to apologize, saying, "I reported it to the police, but they didn't come in time." We realized then that it would be no use pursuing the matter any further. Disgust and anger had to be buried; despair and helplessness took their place.

All our merchandise gone! People must have carried away clothing and linens by the armload. The mayor claimed to have saved some of our property. He brought back a few items and told us that some of our customers had looted our store in order to return the goods to us when we came back. Their good deeds did little to soothe our wounds or to make up for our tremendous losses.

The assassination of a German Embassy official in Paris by a Polish Jew had sparked Nazi anger.

Report From the Municipal Council Meeting
Viernheim, November 11, 1938
It was understandable that the [German] soul rose up and defended itself at the occasion of the murder by the Jewish boy

> in Paris and in justifiable anger retaliated against the Jews for what their international clique did to the German hostland; but it is reprehensible that individuals tried to enrich themselves with the property of the nation. Everything the Jews accumulated in Germany through fraud belongs to the German people. . . . Therefore it is urgently requested that the looted goods . . . be returned immediately to the police. Violations of this notice will be prosecuted.

The Jewish community of Viernheim had been decimated. We were told that all the Jews had been driven together. Then the males had been separated from their families and arrested. Young Brownshirts and civilians came with hatchets, looting and destroying Jewish businesses. People stormed through the shops in droves, carting away whatever they could. The police arrived, not to protect Jewish property or to defend the victims or to arrest the vandals, but to direct traffic. Schoolteachers led their students to the synagogue and set it on fire. The firemen arrived, but only to keep the fire from spreading to neighboring houses. Adults told children to throw rocks at the Jews and their homes.

Never, not even in our worst nightmares, could we have imagined that Germany would descend into such a frenzy of hatred! Six years of poisonous propaganda against the Jews had gradually squeezed us out of German society, and now the fires of national pride had set our world ablaze. The Nazi Party led the charge. The Nazis shattered our synagogues and our lives and dubbed their violent orgy of November 9 and 10, 1938, "Crystal Night" (*Kristallnacht*) because the broken glass of the Jewish shop windows lay sparkling like crystal on the sidewalks and in the streets. To us it was the night of broken lives. On that night, the mad demon of the Middle Ages pogrom returned to take Germany by storm. We knew not when the black clouds of terror would go away.

3

The Oppenheimers should have had ample opportunity to escape well before the pogrom. Earlier, they had applied to emigrate, but there was a long delay in issuing their emigration documents. Why had the papers been held hostage until after that terrible night when they lost virtually everything? Julius and Hugo were forced to sell their plundered business to the city and then hand over the money to the tax office, after which the authorities finally released their emigration papers. By December 1938 both families had received permission to leave for America. I packed their furniture into a number of large containers that stood in the yard. I felt relieved that Doris would have a future in a free country—so we hoped—if it wasn't a trap. As I watched them depart, I stood there numbly—stranded, jobless, the ground snatched out from under my feet. I stayed alone in the big empty apartment, sitting in my little attic room, until the authorities finally ordered me to leave the place.

What to do? Where to go? My hometown of Reichenbach was certainly too small a place in which to hide. Everyone knew me—my arrival would be the news of the day in the close-knit town. The Nazi hunters were on the prowl there too.

Although I longed to know what had become of my family, I decided that it would be best to leave the state of Hesse. Southward lay the state of Baden Württemberg, a different government jurisdiction. There in Pforzheim lived my beloved Laure. It was illegal to leave my home jurisdiction without official permission. But no one knew me in Pforzheim, and I hoped I could hide there. Laure's family welcomed me.

But not too long afterward, the Eckstein's front door shivered under sharp blows. Laure's father struggled to his feet in response to the piercing sound, *"Aufmachen! Polizei!"* The distress in Laure's soft brown eyes mirrored the fear in my own. In an instant I realized how foolish I had been to come to Laure's home.

The police filled the doorway, holding an arrest warrant issued by the Viernheim police for Max Liebster. I went numb. "You're under arrest! You know where you're going. March!"

At the prison, the guard opened a cell, shoved me inside, and slammed the heavy door behind me. His departing footsteps echoed like a knell of doom. The shock of being locked up in prison without a hearing left me dizzy with outrage. I was a German citizen. I expected that eventually someone would come, an official perhaps or a lawyer. Then I would have the chance to explain, "I'm innocent. I'm an honest, hard worker. I'm not a capitalist—I come from a poor Jewish family." I rehearsed my defense: "Ask the customers in Viernheim—they can tell you who I am. My father served in the German army. I'm a German. I have rights!"

Steps came to a halt in front of my cell. An inquisitive eye peered through the peephole. Then the flap at the bottom of the door opened, and food was pushed through by an invisible hand. I did not see a single face the first day or the first week or for many weeks that followed.

A wooden plank attached to one wall served as my chair and my bed. A tiny opening near the high ceiling admitted a single ray of light. I was treated like an animal in a cage. Every day the disembodied hand brought my food and emptied my toilet bucket. The "Aryan" prison guard wouldn't lower himself to speak to an *Untermensch* (subhuman) like me. No voices, no books, no newspapers. No one to ease my heartache and isolation. In total silence, my life plunged into an abyss.

A poster on my cell wall explained how to maintain fitness. It even exhorted male inmates to do push-ups to help cope with their imposed celibacy. I found it ironic that someone apparently cared about the physical condition of the inmates. Like a captive animal, I paced my cell—seven steps long and five steps across. The bars across the unreachable window were superfluous; no one could ever climb up and squeeze himself through the little opening. Through the bars, I could see a patch of sky. It was a major event during the long days when a leaf, snatched by the wind, would dance in front of my window to the world. Sometimes I even glimpsed a bird flying by. For hours I would gaze at the opening that was my only link with freedom.

A sick feeling grew in my stomach whenever I thought about how quickly my world had fallen to pieces. For months after the Jewish community in Viernheim met its tragic end with the arrest of Jewish males and the burning of the synagogue, zealous Nazi hunters continued to stalk their prey. Gestapo (the secret police of the Third Reich, known for their brutality) and police teamed up in tireless pursuit of anyone deemed an enemy of the State. During that time I had lived daily with the debilitating dread of arrest.

Now that my fear of arrest had come to pass, I would repeatedly relive the whole episode leading up to it—the heaps of glass and the devastated shop. I pondered this situation over and over in my mind, not wanting to come to the awful conclusion that I knew deep inside must be true. Could it have been Nazi party members alone who caused the destruction? But how could they have done it all themselves? We had been told of the throngs of people who had violated our store. Had our neighbors deceived us all these years, letting us think they were our friends? Didn't they believe in their holy law and ours, "Thou shalt not steal"? The people of Viernheim were practicing Catholics who faithfully filled the pews every Sunday. Had the seeds of antisemitism lain dormant in their hearts, only to germinate in Nazi soil? How could we have been so blind?

In Reichenbach the synagogue had been sold to "Aryans" in a forced sale in May 1938. That in itself should have been a warning to me. I reproached myself for having been so slow to believe the signs. I tried in vain to fight the creeping feelings of betrayal and abandonment. The pogrom destroyed more than worldly goods—it crushed our confidence. Jewish families became desperate to find a way out. Emigration required papers and money, and most lacked both. Many awaited affidavits from a friend or relative abroad, promising employment and sponsorship.

I tried to remind myself that some people had retained human decency. Julius and Hugo's brother, Leo, had been a popular figure in Viernheim as a member of the local soccer team. Ever since the "Aryanization" of his business, he had been doing forced labor in a factory in Mannheim. Soon after we had fled for the mountains, Leo managed to come to Viernheim to check on the store. Two policemen who knew him urged him to leave as quickly as possible, warning him that all Jewish men would soon be arrested. Leo also learned that we were hiding in the Odenwald Mountains. In retrospect, I wondered if the same two policemen had warned Julius and Hugo to close up the house and escape just before the pogrom. Maybe they were the ones who prevented the mob from ransacking the two apartments above the store. Why didn't more people show courage of that kind? Maybe not all were Nazis, perhaps not all were cowards, but the propaganda had worked.

As I sat in the cold prison cell, I kept reminding myself, "At least I'm between four walls and not in a concentration camp." I consoled myself that some of my family members were better off than I. By the time I was arrested, Ida and Sydney's plan had succeeded—Ida was in West Virginia with Sydney. But I still hadn't heard whether Hanna and Adolf had made it to South America or whether my parents and I could hope for their help.

Would an affidavit for me from the States have set me free? The declaration of war quashed that dream.

September 1, 1939. Hitler's army invaded Poland. Two days later, Poland's allies, England and France, declared war. This didn't bode well for the Jews in Germany. In time of war, "undesirable" people become public enemies overnight. On September 11th, I got my first taste of what it meant to be marked as a foe of the regime. Between my sudden arrest and the declaration of war, I was in a state of shock.

I tried not to wonder why there had been no affidavit, no ticket to freedom, for me. For nine years I had been a member of the Oppenheimer family, and though they had left, I wanted my bonds with them to live on. Haunting doubts flitted in and out of my mind. I tried to swat them away with feeble hopes of rescue. But the silence of passing time slowly eroded what meager hopes I had.

4

With nothing else to fill the endless hours in my cell in the Pforzheim prison, I pondered the troubling descriptions of human conflict and suffering that my father had brought back from the battle lines of the World War. The stories were as incomprehensible to me now as they had been when I was a boy.

Recalling my father's commentary, I was transported back to my childhood. At his cobbler's workbench, Father received veterans, who often came during the long winter evenings to relive their memories from the war. Through a haze of cigarette smoke, I listened from my bed and watched my father's kind face grow bitter. I could see in his eyes a look of profound pain as he lived the battles again and again.

As the men talked, I pictured the primitive shelters and miserable trenches—the rain-soaked soldiers, the moaning wounded, the trembling hands—all awash in flashes of cross fire. I heard that, whenever they could, Jews on both sides of the battlefront recited their prayers in Yiddish, rocking the same way, observing the same Sabbath, following the same Talmud. Then they would fold their *Tefillin* and *Tallith* and again take up guns and bayonets against each other for Germany, Austria, or Russia. I could hardly bear the mental scene of Jew pitted against Jew.

Now, a generation later, all Jews were besieged by a common, vicious enemy.

Where is my God, our God? Why does He allow this? The silence in response to these anguished questions cut me deeply. He who overthrew Sodom and Gomorrah, who drowned Pharaoh and his army—where is He now, the Mighty One of Israel? Why does He not send the Messiah?

I reflected on my religious upbringing, on our holy traditions. My father never left the house without first spending an hour in morning prayer. We never ate unclean food and never failed to keep the Sabbath. Since the time of Abraham, generations of our people have shared a sign of belonging—to one God, to one family. But now the mark of circumcision has been made a stigma that leaves us vulnerable.

Has God abandoned us, or have we abandoned him? The Oppenheimers, and so many others, did only the minimum for God. I too had become lax about my religious observances. Is all this our fault? Is this why He doesn't hear our cries? For centuries we have suffered terrible pogroms. Is it because the Holy One has forsaken us? Our common prayer, *Shema, Yisrael, Adonai Elohenu Adonai echad* ("Listen, O Israel, the Lord our God is one God"); the morning prayer (*shacharit*); and the evening prayer (*ma'ariv*) united all Jews throughout the world. But are we united? Are we one? Then why did we fight one another in the World War? Perhaps we have strayed.

I felt forsaken by everyone—by the customers who had been friendly to me and seemed to respect me, by my friends, by my family, and even by God. I turned my anguished thoughts inward: What have I personally done to deserve God's disapproval? I sit in prison, but not for any mischief or thievery, politics or conspiracy. I am here because I was born a Jew, a part of the Chosen People. And now the Nazis choose my destiny!

The four walls echoed with my questions and returned no answers. Only the sounds of footsteps and rattling keys interrupted the silence. Through the tiny window, I saw the November rains begin to fall. Then the first flakes of snow announced the approaching end of the year.

The door flew open. I instinctively moved away from the opening, as required of inmates. A guard entered the cell and grabbed me roughly. He dragged me out and pushed me in front of another man, in a gray uniform and polished boots and with a pistol on his belt. *"Raus, du Schweinehund!"* (Out, you swine hound!) I panicked, petrified by the thought that I was being led to my execution. I had no recollection of leaving the Pforzheim prison—did I walk?—but the next thing I knew, I stood at the Karlsruhe rail station. A torrent of obscenities spilled out of the mouth of the SS guard.

He shoved me onto a prisoner train with cells made to hold two prisoners each. Looking through the cell peepholes, to his right and to his left, he pushed me down the aisle. The infuriated SS guard finally found a vacant place toward the end of the train. Opening the cell he barked, "You stinking Jew! You will never come back from camp alive!" And with a vicious kick, my fate was sealed!

I lurched forward and landed sprawled on top of a man. I pulled back from him, expecting more abuse. Instead, I saw a smiling gleam in his eyes. It was not what he said but the way he spoke to me that startled me. For more than four months I had not heard a decent word. I had been humiliated and was near collapse at the thought of what lay ahead. This man seemed so serene. How could he sit so calmly in this cage? He must not realize where we are going, I thought. But he is a German. Surely he knows what awaits us in the camps. He must be deliberately blinding himself to reality! But somehow my cellmate's mildness, so puzzling to me at first, refreshed me. His kind manner felt like soothing oil upon my wounds. From here, we would be brothers in suffering as we headed toward our final destiny. I wish I could remember his name.

My cellmate was not a Jew or a so-called *Mischling* (racially mixed individual). He was neither a criminal nor a political dissident. He was an ordinary man whose conscience would not allow him to worship anyone but God. The man belonged to a group called Jehovah's Witnesses, or simply the *Ernste Bibelforscher* (Earnest Bible Students).

The Nazis had banned this small religious group in the early days of the regime. My cellmate had refused to join the Nazi Party and wouldn't use the compulsory greeting *Heil Hitler.* "Worship belongs to God," he told me. To him, saluting Hitler would be like acknowledging him as Germany's savior. Only the Messiah would bring salvation, he said. It startled me to hear a Christian speak of the Messiah.

The man continued to talk. He said that there were thousands like him who had refused to obey Nazi laws that violated their consciences. They wouldn't participate in any work in support of war. He said that love of neighbor moved the Witnesses to face long sentences in prison or camp and even execution rather than compromise their beliefs.

The Nazis even punished Witness women and children. His wife had been sent to a women's concentration camp for raising their five children in their beliefs. He told me sadly that his children had probably been taken to a Nazi reeducation center or perhaps to Nazi "foster" families to liberate them from the corrupt teaching of the *Bibelforscher.* Where were they now? Since their separation, he had received no news of the children. The Gestapo cunningly used this painful silence to try to break him of what he called his personal vow of absolute loyalty to God.

And his wife? "My wife died, probably of starvation," he said quietly, "without ever seeing our children again." I pondered the sad conclusion of his tale and struggled to find words to console this gentle man. But he had more to say. He told me resolutely that he would willingly face the same fate rather than break the vow he had made to God, whom he kept calling "Jehovah." He believed in Jehovah's power to restore life to the dead. Faithfulness and a clear conscience meant more to him than liberty and life. Such noble-sounding ideals! But something in his sincere and steadfast gaze told me he meant every word.

A whistle shrieked, and the train ground to a halt. We heard a commotion outside. Then the guard jerked open our cell door and stomped in with a pair of handcuffs. He cuffed us together and ordered us out. My brave companion remained remarkably calm. He doesn't even fear death, I thought.

At the train station in Frankfurt, an icy wind swept through the rows of handcuffed prisoners. SS officers in crisp uniforms stood by while guards held their guns at the ready and flanked the long column of haggard men. Our grotesque procession snaked through the entire city. Hostile crowds lined the route, anxious to vent their hatred.

"Landesverräter!" (traitor to the nation!)

"Ungeziefer!" (vermin!)

"Criminal!" They screamed, shaking their fists at us. In vain we tried to dodge the missiles hurled at us from every direction. The jeering insults stung my ears and pierced my heart, driving me deeper into despondency. My feet, like lead weights, dragged along mechanically. But my companion kept up a strong pace, determination lining his face. Hope was chained to despair.

The SS marched us to a prison. The cold fear of uncertainty overtook me as we entered the jail. Single cages like those for wild animals stood in small clusters, just out of reach of one another. The guards paced back and forth among the cages. Some prisoners charged to and fro like wild beasts, and others gripped the bars and shook them. The building amplified and echoed the mad ranting. Amid the raging fits and piteous moaning, I imagined I could hear desperate prayers being recited in an undertone.

Were we men or beasts? The utter humiliation of our situation inflicted more pain than the SS lashes. A terrible emptiness left me groping for some kind of comfort. At that moment I spotted my *Bibelforscher* cellmate from the train in one of the cages nearby. He must have sensed that the blows of degradation had wounded me to the core. Through the bars he looked me in the eye and reassured me that to the Almighty, all races are equal. All come from Adam and Eve, and none is superior to the other. He quoted the Torah, the Psalms, and the Prophets, applying the holy words like salve.

In the Pforzheim prison, where I had been completely isolated for weeks and months, time had dragged. Now time seemed to be disjointed and sped by as we kept constantly on the move. Once more we prisoners were handcuffed together and driven like livestock toward the train. The gauntlet awaited us again. The storm of abuse seemed to intensify as the "Aryan" masters saw us "subhumans" being marched off to camp. They sent us away with curses and threats as we were herded back into cells on the icy train. My *Bibelforscher* cellmate and I huddled together for warmth and shared what little food we had.

This German, this Christian, was very different from the Protestants I had known in my hometown of Reichenbach. Neither was he like the Catholic townspeople in Viernheim. Locked with him in the cell, I discovered that he abhorred the worship of idols, which was forbidden by the Law of Moses. He described God the same way I would have: God is one. And to this man, God alone was supreme. He spoke of a coming Messiah and the Golden Age of Peace, which the Messiah's rule would bring to earth. When he explained to me that the Hebrew word "Messiah" was translated in Greek as "Christ," it confused me. I was a Jew—determined to stay a Jew—and for me the word "Christ" tasted bitter. Throughout the ages, the pogroms had all been carried out in the name of Christ. Even when I voiced my objection, my companion didn't turn against me. He kept encouraging me to hold firmly to the Messianic promises of the Scriptures. His comfort is God-sent, I thought. I hoped to spend more days with him after our arrival. But our conversation came to an abrupt end as the train rolled into Sachsenhausen concentration camp.

5

SS guards with rifles trained upon us greeted us with obscenities. They barely kept the bloodthirsty German Shepherd dogs at bay. Each prisoner had to present himself and answer the question, "Why are you here?" My cellmate had hardly spoken the words, "I am Jehovah's Witness," when an SS man kicked him hard and sent him crashing to the frozen ground. Another blow followed and still another as he curled helplessly in a ball, utterly at the mercy of the frenzied guard. Another guard leaped like a beast on the wounded man shouting, "You *Himmelskomiker* (heaven's comic)! You'll only leave this place by the chimney!" I witnessed his ordeal in shock. I looked around and realized that only he had received such a reception. Later, other inmates told me that each Witness received 25 strokes upon arrival. Then all the Witnesses were put in the *Strafblock*, the punishment barracks.

The beatings were administered by *Kapos*, inmate functionaries known for their extreme brutality. Some were as cruel as the SS guards. Not all *Kapos* were cruel, however. Others, fighting for their own survival, showed zeal in their duties because they were under pressure from the SS guards to do so.

The guards herded us prisoners to the shower and disinfection barracks. A *Kapo*, under SS oversight, watched us strip off our clothes, and then another prisoner roughly shaved every hair from our bodies. Naked like a worm, I felt stripped of all vestiges of dignity. My prison number and a symbol had to be sewn on my jacket. A red triangle pointing down and on it a yellow one pointing up made a Star of David and identified me as a political prisoner and a Jew.

The Jews were kept together in special barracks under murderous conditions. A single straw-filled sack served as the bed for four prisoners, which provided only enough space for the prisoners to lie on their sides, packed like sardines. The barracks echoed with loud cursing over kicks in the face by dirty feet, the din occasionally punctuated by the screams of those tormented by nightmares. When an inmate returned from the latrine, he had to force himself into place again among the tightly packed bodies.

I had arrived at the concentration camp with a terrible and frightening image, gleaned from Sydney's account of Buchenwald, of what lay within the gates. As horrific as my vision of camp life was, it far understated reality. In my first days and nights, I saw things far worse than anything Sydney had described: walking skeletons, dazed and mute except for an occasional burst of maniacal laughter, and SS men acting as perverse gods, beating weak, pitiable men for the least infraction. This was hell. Especially was it so for the Jews, whose barracks were even more horrible than those of other prisoners. I was convinced that Sachsenhausen concentration camp was part of the machinery to accomplish the destruction of the Jews.

Roll call rang out before dawn. Prisoners scrambled to line up in precise rows. The checking of the roster dragged out interminably. The dead from the previous night, stacked in front of the barracks, completed the count. When anyone came up missing, the search went on for hours.

The German, non-Jewish inmates were formed into *Kommandos* (work details). They left in formation with a marching song. When the exhausted work detail returned, the evening roll call began. If an inmate could not be found, the guards went wild. The counting began anew—the darkness fell hard, and the cold tortured us as we stood shivering in the mounting snow —the counting and recounting stealing the hours of the night.

Blizzard winds extinguished flickers of life in Sachsenhausen. The list of the living grew shorter each day. Ears and noses fell off, broken like glass.

My toes and fingers froze. "No medical care for Jews. Urinate on them!" they told me. I did. It was the only treatment available.

Here was the renowned German orderliness—prisoners standing in neat rows, and no one with the right to ease himself when nature called. Machine guns and searchlights held everything under control—or almost everything. The heavens lay out of reach of the guard towers. Running clouds, twinkling stars, and the bright sun brought me consolation. "Blessed be the name of the Eternal," the rabbi in Reichenbach had said. "All creation bears witness to the greatness of God." I could hear his chant in the synagogue. But my eyes returned earthward to behold the misery around me. I knew that this could not be the work of the Eternal One, whose name I blessed. My *Bibelforscher* cellmate had said it well, "The whole world is under the power of evil. The book of Job calls him Satan, he who causes our sobbing and outcries."

Jews were not allowed to work in Sachsenhausen itself. The SS had other things in mind for us. Barking commands blared from the loudspeakers, summoning the Jews. SS men and *Kapos* watched and waited for even the smallest infraction. When they found it, then came the call, "Barrack number so-and-so, *Raus! Strafsport!*" (Out! Punishment sports!) It was the dreaded *Sachsengruss* (Saxon greeting)—crouch down with hands behind the head, with only the toes touching the ground, and then the order: *Up! Down! Up! Down!* How can they jump when they are so weak? Elderly Jews were beaten without mercy. *Up! Down! Up! Down!* When a man gave out, the guard ordered him to roll back and forth on his stomach in the snow, in the rain, or in a puddle of mud. As the exhausted prisoner lay still, gasping for breath, an SS boot came down on his neck, forcing him to breathe in whatever was on the ground, whether it was water or the slime that spread over the roll call grounds.

The SS guards had their fun forcing the Jews to do "sports" for hours in all kinds of weather. The list of the living shrank still further. Destruction through sports efficiently eliminated the old, the weak, and the exhausted without bloodshed.

Each morning we had to pile up the straw mattresses in our barracks. With nothing to sit on, we squatted on the ice-cold floor or leaned against the wall, buried in our thoughts. Veterans warned the new prisoners, "You haven't seen anything yet. Just wait." I grew even more anxious. Did they have to add to our burdens with hints of greater terrors yet to come? The prayers of devout prisoners prompted indignant remarks by the less reverent: "Why pray to a God who has sold us into the hands of torturers? Why praise Him for what we receive, beatings and kicks? Why thank Him for our hunger? He is the Almighty in whose hands we are, and we are skeletons waiting for the crematorium! For what should we exalt Him?"

Another prisoner expired. We dragged him outside to be counted with the living so the roll call number would be complete. A cauldron carried by two prisoners contained our meal of turnip soup. The men lined up. The clever ones stayed to the back of the line, hoping to get the bottom part of the watery soup, where a few shreds of turnip lay. Each of us had a metal bowl and a spoon. Fights broke out over the unfair distribution. The prisoner in charge of the barrack beat the offenders to restore order.

Outside, a desperate inmate ran into the electric fence, ending his misery. No guard tried to shoot him; the electricity did the job. It meant one less on the roll call roster. Others followed him ever so regularly, choosing the quicker way instead of lying on straw sacks waiting for death.

I continued to treat my frozen fingers and toes with the tonic of my own urine, using strips of my shirt as bandages. Slowly the frostbite healed, and gangrene missed claiming me as a victim. Little by little, the thermometer rose above the freezing mark. The snows melted, but the rains took their place. Our soggy clothes never dried, and *Strafsport* made it even worse.

Wearing white gloves, the SS guard stepped into the barracks to check the beams. If the glove came back soiled, he punished the entire group, either by *Strafsport* or by denying us food. We seldom passed inspection.

"There is another Liebster in that barrack," someone told me. My family name was so rare that I had to see about it. I entered the barrack and peered behind the pile of straw sacks. The sight was unbearable. An endless row of living corpses lay helpless, neglected, and abandoned, waiting only for death. "Where is Liebster?" I asked. A man with a ghastly ashen face and huge eyes slowly turned his head and stared up at me. Suddenly, his eyes filled with tears.

"Max! My son, Max!"

Who was this whisper of a man? I barely recognized him. My father's legs had swollen so much that he could not stand. He broke down sobbing and so did I. Day after day, I went to him whenever I could. He lay quiet except when he could muster the strength to utter a prayer, *"Shema, Yisrael, Adonai Elohenu Adonai echad."* Father told me that Hanna had only been successful in securing papers for Mother to emigrate. He didn't know if Mother had made it. He had shut out his memories; he had no hope, no past, no future. I sat by his side in silence. Tears streamed down our shriveled faces. We kept barely afloat in a sea of forsaken souls.

One day Father rose up and laid his hands gently upon my head to bestow a blessing. He implored the Almighty to remember me and make me like Ephraim and Manasseh. His voice became inaudible; sobs drowned out his benediction. I bowed my head in prayer and in grief. He lay down, and the last flicker of life disappeared from his eyes. He was 60 years old. Father reached the end of his suffering, leaving me anguished and alone.

"Carry your father to the crematorium. It's the last service you can perform for him." Did the *Kapo* intend to deepen my sorrow, or did he have noble intentions? His order left me paralyzed. With no help, no consolation, how could I bear it? Where the strength came from, I do not know. I lifted my father and swung his shrunken body over my shoulders. His head dangled against my back while I held his legs tightly to my chest. His body would not have to join the pile outside the barrack, waiting to be stacked like wood in the truck. The thought gave me scant comfort amidst the deepest sorrow I could ever know.

The stabbing pains in my heart spurred me on. I wept bitterly as my load grew heavier. The walk from the barrack to the crematorium stretched on without end. I wanted to give up, but the SS man in the guard tower would have been only too happy to unload his rifle on us. I kept moving somehow, despite an inward turmoil resisting my forward motion: What is the use of living? Why not go with Father into the oven? When I reached the incinerators, the guards told me to deposit my father upon a huge heap of naked skeletons. The prisoners' uniforms were removed and put back into circulation—nothing was wasted.

A stupefying stench arose from the dead who had to wait before cremation—there were more bodies than the ovens could handle. Here, in front of the ghastly heaps of dead, I felt that I deposited my own life as I let down my beloved father from my shoulders. I could have cried out in pain except for the numbness that overtook me. I could not bear to picture my father's countenance, his expression erased by hunger, pain, and despair.

Released from my load, I walked away from the crematorium as quickly as I could. But I carried the weight on my shoulders still; it would be there forever. I had no tears left. Drowning in endless grief, I caught sight of the rolling clouds. My father's blessing rang in my ears, and so did the words of my cellmate. God had shown the prophet Daniel that some day the coming Messiah would awaken the dead. The final victory would belong to him and not to Death.

Following the perimeter of Sachsenhausen, I passed near a camp within the camp, where so-called dangerous inmates were isolated. A voice over the loudspeaker repeatedly warned that prisoners would get 25 strokes for stepping over a white brick line that surrounded the small cluster of barracks. The loudspeaker also carried warnings of similar punishment for anyone who tried to talk with the *Bibelforscher*. Was my cellmate in there? What makes these people so dangerous to the Nazi regime? Is the Bible such a subversive book? I felt sad that I had no way of getting in touch with these men, whose faith seemed unsettling to the mighty SS. The two weeks I had spent caged together with one of them had brought me a faint ray of light. Thanks to the SS threats, the forbidden barracks stirred in me a shred of hope once again. I longed for a Bible.

As a solitary man, I sat among people whose spirits had been crushed by the horrors of life in the camp. Veterans died, new ones sat immobile in silence, and I had to bear my bereavement alone. No one expected a different fate—we would all find release only through the chimney. I saw dozens follow that route every day. Roll call claimed just as many victims under the burning sun as it did during the howling winter gale. The grounds dried out, leaving a dusty layer of slag that rose in a choking cloud. The *Strafsport* was even more murderous in the blazing heat. But the exercise I had done at the Pforzheim prison had built up my strength, and my cellmate had nursed my spirit and given me the will to fight off a mental breakdown. In the dark tunnel of despair, I clung to a faint beacon of light.

They called my number: 14982. Report to camp headquarters. Terror of the unknown gripped me. Camp life was so cruel and capricious. The mere failure to take off one's cap and stand at attention resulted in a stiff penalty. The guards had their standard daily punishments, kicking and beating without mercy, and once in a while a random shooting. Prisoners had to stand at the camp gate for an entire day without moving. Or the SS guards might order a *Kapo* to mete out a whipping of 25 strokes on the naked buttocks. Some prisoners were subjected to the *Marterpfahl*—with hands tied behind their backs, they hung by the wrists for hours until their shoulder muscles tore and their own body weight pulled their arms from the sockets.

A prison stood next to camp headquarters. In that place death sentences were carried out by public hanging. I was told that shortly before I arrived at the camp, a platform with a wall had been erected. All the many thousands of prisoners had to assemble to watch a man brought in to face a firing squad. He had refused to be drafted. There were also "transports" to unknown places. I had managed to avoid punishment to this point, but now it was my turn.

6

Three years had elapsed since "Crystal Night." I stood stripped of my rights and my dignity, exposed to the whim of the "Master Race." On the main gate of Sachsenhausen, one could read the mocking words forged in iron, *"ARBEIT MACHT FREI"* (work makes you free). Other young Jews had also been summoned on this cold November day. An SS officer told us that we had been chosen to go to a work camp called Neuengamme.

We agreed among ourselves that working would be better than having to squat for hours in the miserable barracks. The guards never seemed to tire of finding ever more sadistic tortures to pass the time. Our work detail might escape the deadly *Strafsport* exercises. Nevertheless, we knew that the SS and the *Kapos* would drive us to our last drop of blood.

Neuengamme; November 19, 1941. Different camp, same routine. Here too they shaved us completely and doused us with a disinfectant that stung our armpits and private parts. Afterward, we had to run naked in the cold to the next barrack, where a hot shower and dressing room awaited us. As in Sachsenhausen, the *Kapos* here wore the green triangles of criminals or the red triangles of political prisoners, mostly Communists. They also wore the same twisted smirk, which told us that the more ways they found to brutalize us, the more favors they could get from the SS guards.

Finally we were fit to be ushered in to the *Kommandant*. Standing at attention with caps off, 30 young German Jews with stone faces listened tensely to the haranguing from our new taskmaster. We understood only too well that crushing labor awaited us. "These 30 Jews to the barracks of the *Bibelforscher*," he bellowed with contempt. "They both have the same God!" At once, a flicker of warmth crept into my sagging heart.

As we stepped into our assigned barrack, our mouths dropped open in disbelief. The whole place was scrubbed meticulously clean. The bunks had bran mattresses—one to each man. What a luxury to be able to stretch out and turn over at will! We felt human again, at least in our bunks. No more sharing a straw sack with the sick, dying, and dead. We were told that in the short time between the morning bell and the roll call, we had to "build" the bed—carefully flattening the top and forming sharp edges, with the blanket folded neatly on top. The prisoner in charge of this barrack warned us that one unkempt bunk would mean punishment for all.

It took a little while before it dawned on me what else made this barrack markedly different—the atmosphere. An air of respect and cooperation replaced the stealing and loud quarreling that normally filled the barracks. Somehow camp life had not robbed these men of their dignity and human kindness.

Being the youngest, I claimed a top bunk. In the next bunk over was a *Bibelforscher*, Ernst Wauer. After work, when we could rest in our bunks, he and I talked. Many of the inmates in this barrack wore the purple triangle of the *Bibelforscher*, or Jehovah's Witnesses. They seemed to have some authority to make certain rules in the barrack.

The work routine quickly overtook our lives. The *Kapos* cruelly drove the 300-man Dove Elbe work unit on a forced march every morning to one of two distant work sites, the Kaimauer Canal or the Klinker-Werk brick factory. Under a shower of blows, our work unit left the roll call at 7:00 a.m., marching in time to the work songs they sang. "Left-right, left-right," in rows of five, marching for over an hour. At 6:30 p.m. we returned, loaded down with the dead, trembling with exhaustion. Everyone had to be present for the evening roll call, even the corpses.

As we anticipated, the work assignment demanded the impossible of healthy men, let alone walking skeletons. We had to excavate the Kaimauer Canal, enlarging it to allow barge traffic. The huge crater had several levels. Some prisoners dug trenches and laid out small planks on top of the mud. Others, like me, pushed wheelbarrows. We formed a human assembly line in this clockwork system. The rhythm of labor was calculated so that no one could stop. Prisoners were lined up along the planks, and each in turn would dump a shovelful of sand into my wheelbarrow as I pushed it across the planks. In the deepest part of the hole, I had to push through the wet sand with all my might. The last shovelful filled the heavy wheelbarrow to the brim. I held the handles of the wheelbarrow in a death grip, knowing that if I stumbled or let my backbreaking load tip over, it could be all over for me. Even a brief pause to catch a breath could attract the ire of the SS or the merciless strokes of a *Kapo* who continually shouted *"schnell, schnell!"* (faster, faster!).

The skies over Neuengamme frequently poured down water, mirroring the gloomy terrain below. We spent the workday soaked to the skin. Our shoes were falling apart, with nothing at hand to repair them. Our stiff hands reluctantly grasped our tools. Buttoning and unbuttoning our thin, tattered jackets was a major feat. When nature called, we perched precariously on a plank above a trench. Easing nature became a serious and frightening undertaking because falling into the latrine meant sure death by drowning in excrement.

We struggled just to hold the spoons for the meager soup that was distributed at noon from huge cauldrons at the work site. The nagging pains of hunger mingled with frustration as the aggressive ones pushed us forward once again so they could be last in line and get the few pieces of kohlrabi lying at the bottom of the pot.

We lived for Sundays, when we could finally take refuge from the slave drivers. What a contrast between the weekday routine and the Sunday meal in our barrack! The soup tasted the same, and the pains of starvation still nagged at us. But how different was the distribution of the food. Men stood quietly waiting their turn, while the one ladling out the soup stirred the pot before dipping out each bowlful.

One day an announcement blared over the loudspeaker. The *Kommandant* said that we should expect a special visit. We had to clean and polish everything in our barracks—floor, tables, and even ourselves. The next day, flowerpots appeared on the barrack windowsill. The soup cauldron even had some pieces of meat swimming in a savory broth. The high-ranking visiting official stomped through the camp, grunting his satisfaction over the great accomplishments of the *Kommandant,* who had civilized us prisoners, the *Untermenschen* (subhumans). The next day, our normal life resumed—complete with rotten-turnip soup.

On occasion, an SS man stepped into our barrack for surprise inspection. We jumped to attention until he shouted *"Weitermachen!"* (resume your work!). Seldom would he find a reason to punish us. Not that he was reluctant to do so. But the *Bibelforscher* believed it their Christian duty to obey the camp regulations. I found it rather curious that, on the one hand, they would usually follow the camp rules to the letter, even if no one supervised them. On the other hand, when they decided that a rule was against God's law, they dug in their heels like stubborn children and refused to obey. Only this was no game. The SS threatened them, tortured them, and worse. But no amount of abuse could make them give in.

For instance, I found out that the execution that had been the talk of Sachsenhausen when I first arrived was that of a purple triangle. His name was August Dickmann. Three days after the start of the war, Dickmann had been ordered to sign his military induction slip—a ticket out of the living hell. Yet, he refused to join the military. For him, killing was out of the question. He believed in a commandment I knew well, "Thou shalt not murder." The whole camp had to gather on the assembly grounds to watch him die by firing squad.*

The *Bibelforscher* Ernst Wauer, my barrack companion, had been in Sachsenhausen since the spring of 1939 and had witnessed the public execution. He told me that after Dickmann was shot, the *Kommandant* was sure that the 400 purple triangles looking on would give up their faith on the spot. They could have signed a document renouncing their religion. When none of them did, the SS tortured them all with *Strafsport* until every single one collapsed from exhaustion. The SS beat them with sticks and kicked them as they lay immobile on the ground. Still, on that day not one purple triangle renounced his faith. No wonder that months later the whole camp still talked about the incident.

When I arrived in Sachsenhausen four months after Dickmann's execution, I myself saw the brutal SS welcome that awaited my *Bibelforscher* cellmate. I heard that the purple triangles were routinely given 25 strokes just because of their faith. Or the SS blasted them with a water hose and then made them stand in the freezing weather for hours. Many purple triangles who entered Sachsenhausen during the frigid winter of 1939/40 didn't survive the first few weeks. My cellmate from the train probably perished along with about 100 other *Bibelforscher* that winter.

Nearly two years had passed since I had shared the train ride with a man of faith. Now, here in Neuengamme, I found myself living among others like him. With the SS so bent on breaking the purple triangles, how could it be that some of them were still alive

---

* A memorial plaque for Dickmann was unveiled at Sachsenhausen concentration camp on September 18, 1999.

after years in camp? Some had prisoner numbers with only three digits—proof that they were among the "old prisoners," the first to be incarcerated. The purple triangle in a bunk nearby had survived prison and camp since 1934. Some had been in Neuengamme since it had first been turned into a camp. Ernst Wauer had been in custody since September 1936. I felt blessed to live with men who loved God more than they loved themselves. The camp *Kommandant* had shouted: "Put them with the *Bibelforscher*—they have the same God!" The *Kommandant* would never know what a favor he did for me.

Ernst Wauer was like a living Bible. Every evening he would quote texts from the Psalms and the Prophets. He retold the inspiring stories I had heard in my childhood. Joshua courageously obeyed God's command to lead Israel to the Promised Land. Wauer assured me that the greater Joshua would soon come to lead us to the more glorious Promised Land—Paradise on earth. Wauer asked, "Did not God promise Abraham that 'through your seed all nations will be blessed'?" He also told me I should forget the "curse" that so-called Christians said we Jews still carried because our ancestors had spilled Jesus' blood. God would not be bound by the curses of men. He would judge all men with righteousness. It lay within the hands of each one to choose whether to follow the right path or not. Those who exercised faith in God would one day be the victors, even as Father Abraham was.

Wauer and the others certainly seemed unshakable in their beliefs. Though wracked with pain in that sea of horror, they struggled daily to live by the laws of God, which we Jews called the *mitzvot*. Their strength of conviction shored up my desperate heart. But even as my despair slowly melted away in the glow of the Word, my body continued to weaken. Hunger, hard labor, and exposure leeched my remaining energy. I felt myself reaching my limit. I was ready to believe that a resurrection and a Golden Age lay ahead, but I still found it hard to face death at age 27. Blizzard conditions and freezing rain cut short many lives. SS bullets and killer dogs did away with others. Diarrhea and starvation took still more. I wondered in which incarnation Death would come for me.

Then one day an inmate let me in on a secret. Two purple triangles had been assigned to feed and tend the Angora rabbits that the SS raised in a building near the camp gate. These two *Bibelforscher* undertook an extremely risky operation. If a prisoner in the barrack showed signs of starvation and they felt he could be trusted not to give them away, they would set a time for him to come by to pick up food meant for the rabbits. To my great surprise, someone quietly told me to go and see the purple triangle named Johe. On certain evenings and on Sundays, I would slip over to the rabbit cages and quickly stuff my pockets with vegetable peelings. This rabbit food was a delicacy, far more nourishing than the so-called kohlrabi soup, in which the kohlrabi was all but invisible. These two men risked themselves several times for me. Slowly, I started to recuperate. My steps became steadier in the nonstop work of pushing the heavy wheelbarrow through the sand and over the uneven planks.

With the help of Wauer and his friends, I survived my second winter in camp. The days seemed to last forever; yet before I knew it, a third winter was upon us. One morning at roll call, we saw barbed-wire enclosures erected between the barracks. Corralled like animals inside, hundreds of young Russian soldiers stood huddled together in the mud, battered by the icy rain and deprived of food and water. Their terrorized, ghostlike faces had lost all human expression. These young men met an early and, to me, an unnecessary death—simply because they had been born Russian and had been put in uniform. How could hundreds of prisoners of war be liquidated in just a few days? I could not put out of my mind the subsequent scene of trucks piled high with their dead bodies. I realized that alongside the Jews, countless non-Jews suffered from the expansion politics of the Third Reich.

My father's war stories had impressed upon me the senseless-ness of armed conflict and the hypocrisy of prayers—recited on both sides in a conflict!—that invoke God's blessing on deadly weapons. Yet, the futility of battle paled in comparison with the wanton slaughter I now saw before my eyes. And still some religious leaders had the audacity to claim God's support. The German chaplains cheered on the "Aryan" armies in their conquest of land for *Lebensraum* (living space). They preached the new gospel: the Nazi doctrine of the Super Race and the Survival of the Fittest. How many lives would yet be wasted for this madness?

Purple triangles such as August Dickmann had sacrificed their lives rather than share in the insanity of war. The more I contem-

---

Ernst Wauer (1902–1993). Ernst Wauer was born to staunch Lutheran parents in the Berlin suburb of Charlottenburg. As a soldier during World War I, Wauer became disillusioned by the position of his church in the conflict. He joined the *Bibelforscher* in 1935 despite the Nazi ban. In 1936 he was arrested and imprisoned, leaving behind a wife and two children. He spent one year in solitary confinement. Thereafter, Wauer went to the Neusustrum camp (Emsland). In 1939 the camp *Kommandant* asked Wauer if he had changed his beliefs. When Wauer replied that he had not, the *Kommandant* ordered him transferred to Sachsenhausen concentration camp.

An underground network among the 400 Jehovah's Witnesses circulated Scripture texts and pages of Watch Tower literature that had been smuggled into the camp. Wauer was among the organizers. In spring 1940, Wauer was transported to Neuengamme concentration camp, which was still under construction. When he received a temporary assignment as a typist in the *Kommandant's* office, he risked severe punishment to type copies of Bible literature to circulate among Witness prisoners. There were 70 Witnesses in Neuengamme in 1943.

In 1944 the Gestapo raided the Witness barracks and discovered the hidden material. Wauer was subject to three days of torture and interrogation, after which he was transferred to Schandelah camp near Braunschweig. Near the end of the war, the SS loaded the inmates of Schandelah onto a train bound for Lübeck, where the SS intended to force the prisoners to board ships that would be sunk. On the way to Lübeck, though, the train broke down.

Wauer returned home to learn that his wife Eva had died of an illness, and his two children were in the custody of their grandparents. The physical damage from the three-day torture session affected Wauer for the rest of his life.

plated the purple triangles, the more I saw the logic of their ways. It seemed to me that they were a model of how civilized humans ought to behave.

A rumor circulated that all the Jews would be sent to an extermination camp. It turned out to be true. When they heard the news, Ernst Wauer and the other *Bibelforscher* gathered around me and wept. For nearly two years, we had fought together to survive. They had helped me in so many ways, and our common suffering had forged strong bonds of friendship. After such sweet camaraderie, the separation would be heartrending. I assured them that I looked forward to the resurrection to come during the Age of Messiah. The Jews were named for Judah, whose offspring became the leading tribe in Israel and whose name meant "praise Jehovah."* I stood ready to live up to the meaning of the name Jew by putting full faith in the promise given by the patriarch Jacob to his son Judah, from whose tribe the Messiah would come.

The Jews were crammed onto a train. Mocking SS guards prophesied that we would soon be reduced to ashes or a bar of soap, that we would be gassed like vermin. The cattle car echoed with ceaseless moaning and lamentation. Yet, on the transport from Neuengamme to Auschwitz, my outlook differed immensely from the utter hopelessness I had felt three years before on the journey from prison to the Sachsenhausen camp. I knew, of course, that this was the last stretch of the road to annihilation. But my faith was stronger than ever in the God of Abraham, Isaac, and Jacob, the God of the living and not of the dead. I hoped He would give me the strength to face my fate.

---

*Genesis 29:35 states: "She conceived again and bore a son, and declared, 'this time I will praise the LORD.' Therefore, she named him Judah."— *Tanakh—The Holy Scriptures.*

7

Auschwitz; October 23, 1942. Upon our arrival on the rails of Auschwitz-Birkenau, we saw entire families coming from the East. Sheer terror had carved deep lines in their faces. On the train platform, we saw husbands and wives wrenched apart while their children shrieked in fear. Even though our emotions had long since been numbed, we found it hard to witness this atrocious sight. With whips and dogs, the SS guards herded the people to their destiny. The very young and very old were loaded onto trucks to relieve them of the long walk, or so the SS told them. We scoffed at the notion that our tormentors suddenly felt compassion for their victims. We had lived under their lash in the German camps too long. Why should it be any different in Poland?

Mass murder took on a terrifying reality in Auschwitz. A paralyzing dread began driving away all my rational thoughts. The nauseating stench of burning flesh saturated the air. Chimneys swathed in haze heaved smoke and ash into the sky. These signals of doom taunted the living as efficiently as they dispersed the remains of the dead. My group received a temporary reprieve: We would be sent to work in Auschwitz-Buna. (There were several camps close together called Auschwitz. Auschwitz-Buna is best known for the factories that employed slave laborers.) But first, of course, we *Untermenschen* had to be deloused. We lined up in alphabetical order by last name, but the next instant, the brief reference to our identities vanished. For almost three years, I had been just a number. And now I watched my left arm as a needle was deftly maneuvered to form the number 6, followed by 9733. And so, I mused, I am now tattooed like an animal headed for the slaughter.

The bluish numbers reminded me daily that the end would not be postponed for long. The interval between arrival and departure through the chimney seemed to grow shorter and shorter. Yet, somehow I escaped the inexorable reality we saw fulfilled day after day. Like the other laborers, I grasped frantically like a drowning man at the hope of rescue.

As had the slaves of ancient Egypt, we would build factories for the modern Pharaoh. I tried to console my companions by telling them about the prophecy of Daniel, which foretold the downfall of the cruel dictatorship. Ernst Wauer had told me that oppression would not last for decades, as it had under the Egyptian yoke. But the harsh reality was that for my Jewish comrades and me, salvation might delay too long. A battle took shape within me. Grinding misery and macabre scenes of death warred with my hope for a divine Day of Reckoning. Even as I tried to share my conviction that our bondage would soon end, I found myself sliding back into the mire of despair.

From the outside, the barracks looked no different than those in Neuengamme, but the atmosphere inside was completely different. Here in Auschwitz-Buna, I quickly learned that if I did not want to eat my bread ration, distributed in the evenings, I would have to hide it. Driven by hunger, some turned to thievery, depriving their comrades of food for a full 24 hours. Similarly, those who carelessly left their good shoes unattended returned to find old battered ones in their place. Violence bred violence. How I missed Ernst Wauer!

Newcomers arrived daily, mostly from the ghettos of Poland. They brought with them fresh stories of heartbreak and misery.

When they found a former acquaintance, they would shed tears together as they reminisced about all that had been lost. Polish became the main language in the barrack, besides Yiddish. I could barely follow the conversations in my poor Yiddish. But I didn't need to understand the words to know what they had been through. The expressions of pain on their faces told me clearly enough. The ceaseless din in the barrack accentuated my loneliness. I never met any of my former acquaintances. Were they all gone?

The I. G. Farben Company planned to erect a factory in Buna. We had to build it with our bare hands under the most barbaric conditions. Steel beams were unloaded from railcars by sheer manpower. Hundreds of hands pulling on ropes would haul the steel onto wooden beams. The *Kapos* thrashed us more harshly than the SS men, as they garnered points for providing brutal entertainment. The monstrous work left many totally spent. When the guards thought that the exhausted inmates were no longer fit for work, they had the prisoners gassed and sent to the Auschwitz smokestack.

My crew was assigned to erect the steel framework for the I. G. Farben factory. Another prisoner and I had to sit on opposite ends of a girder as a crane hoisted it more than ten meters high. Suspended in midair, beaten by driving rain, icy wind, or burning sun, we had to grasp part of the existing structure, pull ourselves toward it, and bolt the girder to it. Then we climbed down the ladder and began the cycle again, all under watchful SS eyes.

We too had to be watchful. Our taskmaster could never be satisfied. The SS guard was an ordinary man turned devil, with the right to shoot on the spot anyone who displeased him. When we thought he wasn't looking, we stole glances at his eyes. If they were glazed over from a night of drinking, or twinkled perversely over a new mutilation or another murder, we had to kowtow to the master all the same. It was especially dangerous to get close to him or attract his attention at those times. Hard work and obsequiousness might buy survival for that day from the overlord.

The whole key to not getting shot was to keep a low profile. This survival strategy depended heavily on reading the mood of the SS guards and acting decisively when we sensed danger. The capriciousness and brutality of the guards could come out at any time for little or no reason. It became an obsession: Read the signs, stay downwind, keep out of the rifle scope. This perilous waltz filled our days and left no room for meditation on loftier topics. When the macabre dance stopped each evening, we dragged ourselves back, marching in formation, to roll call and a mouthful of bread.

> A shout of joy resounds across the field:
> Hail you, my Führer, Germany's shelter and hero!
> Continue on to sow; we are your seedlings!
> Wherever you plant us, we'll ripen into deeds.
> —*"The Day of Victory" (Nazi song)*

One day an SS guard recognized my accent. We were from the same region of Germany. He came from Mannheim, not far from Viernheim. Whenever possible he had a word with me, even though camp rules prohibited ordinary conversation between guards and prisoners. His inner turmoil drove him to bridge the chasm between *Übermenschen* (superhumans) and *Untermenschen* (subhumans). He wore wretched chains of his own. As a young boy, he had embraced the ideology of a greater Germany. He grew up strong and handsome and set out in uniform as an SS conqueror, bound by unconditional oath to his Messiah, the Führer. In those early years, little did he realize what his Savior would demand of him. Now that Germany's "invincible" army had suffered one defeat after another, he saw the showdown at hand.

"I feel as if I were on a runaway train hurtling downhill," he lamented to me. "It will crash without fail. But if I try to jump off,

I'll be shot. You, Max, have a greater chance of survival than I do." His eyes looked infinitely sad. He struggled with the crushing burden of his conscience and his bitter disillusionment. His confession broadened my insight and evoked a kind of pity for the misled. I wondered how many swaggering SS princes were nothing more than broken men in uniform. It occurred to me that these miserable creatures were blind to the fact that they were not so different from their enemies, the Russians, whom they had killed by the hundreds in Neuengamme. Political ideologies had turned ordinary men into mortal foes, and now they were chained by their duty to act as the executioners of their nation's ambition.

Until the day I heard this guard speak with the accent of my home, I had completely blocked out my past. The ordeal of Sachsenhausen had virtually erased my former identity. Who could have predicted that a conversation with an SS man would revive old memories? Occasionally, the Mannheim SS man would say a word to me, but I had to beware. I knew how a human face could turn hideous without warning. In an instant, naïve trust could bring one under the boot. My friends in Neuengamme had taught me to be discreet and to keep a low profile. To betray even a hint of emotion, whether sympathy or disdain, in front of an SS man could be deadly.

Prisoners found ways to exercise a certain morbid freedom. Cigarette addicts swapped their bread ration to feed their habit, even if it hastened their transformation into a *Muselmann*— the name for those who had reached their last days.

Dr. Josef Mengele, one of the SS doctors assigned to Auschwitz, or others on his staff occasionally paid a visit to Buna to make a *Selektion* of those too weak to work. What kind of doctor was this who perverted the healing skills beyond recognition? Rumors of his grisly medical experiments rippled through the camp. During *Selektion,* men would pass naked in front of him. The remaining work capacity of an inmate was carefully calculated by how shriveled his buttocks were. The tattoo numbers of the chosen men were written down. That night, some of the condemned would sit numbly, oblivious to their fate. Others gave way to madness. Their tormented wailing filled the barracks until a special truck came to take them away to the main camp of Auschwitz-Birkenau, never to return. The omnipresent stench of burning flesh reminded us that the crematoriums never lacked for fodder.

We feared diarrhea as much as *Selektion* (whether by Mengele or an SS bullet). Exhaustion and exposure only aggravated the breakdown of a body fed on rotten-turnip soup. For almost five years, I had managed to dodge this killer, but my turn finally came. My strength drained away rapidly, and the wings of death circled overhead. I made it back to camp only with the help of two boys who supported me by the armpits. During roll call I wept and trembled. Suddenly the Mannheim SS man appeared and ordered me to present myself at his office the following morning. I survived the night, and instead of being taken away in the morning as a *Muselmann,* I received a work assignment in the SS mess hall.

"My" SS man knew I would be free to pick through the leftovers from the meals to supplement my rations. Indeed, the leftovers helped me back on my feet. It also helped a great deal to work inside, where I was protected from the elements. Yet, the job held its dangers. Previously, I had always managed to keep out of sight of the *Kapos* and SS men, but it was impossible to remain inconspicuous here. They even made me a foreman. My tattoo was used to identify me and my work detail of nine. Going and coming, we passed through the gate where I had to say, "No. 69733 plus nine." If any were missing, I had to answer for it, and if anyone died I had to bring the body along as proof. Each time I could say "69733 plus nine," I lived another day. My life depended on those nine people. If one escaped, I would be hanged.

Unlike the random shootings at the work site, a hanging was an orchestrated ceremony. The SS took special pains to make sure we took in the full impact of their show. One day after work, we arrived at the camp to find three gallows erected in the plaza. We all had to gather for roll call, and three manacled prisoners were led in. The *Kommandant* read the verdict, adding, "This is a warning and an example to all."

He ordered the condemned, two men and a small boy biting his lip, to stand on chairs. All the prisoners had to look toward them. The SS and *Kapos* would beat anyone who tried to turn his head or close his eyes to avoid the spectacle. The nooses went around the victims' necks. The two men shouted, "Long live liberty, long…" Three SS men tipped the chairs; the bodies fell. The loudspeaker blared, "Bare your heads!" Like a well-oiled machine, the caps came off. "Cover your heads!" The caps flew back on.

All the prisoners had to walk past the dangling bodies to contemplate their dull eyes and blue tongues. Next to me stood the brother of the unfortunate boy. As we passed in front of the gallows, he burst out in anguished howling. His little brother's tongue was pink, and his body still jerked horribly with life. We returned to our barracks with bitter tears.

Though I was assigned to the mess hall, I was also sent to work in other places throughout the SS quarters. One day I had to bring an SS bicycle to the repair shop. Without thinking, I put one foot on the pedal and scooted along, unaware that a *Kapo* would seize the opportunity to prove his efficiency and earn himself a double ration of bread or cigarettes. He pointed me out to an SS guard and snarled, "That dirty Jew dares to step on the bicycle pedal and defile it." I was ordered to report.

I dreaded the agony of merciless strokes, as well as the torturous aftermath. Over the years, I had seen so many victims who could not heal from floggings. Bloody pus seeped through their trousers until they finally perished in misery. I was but skin and bones, destined for the same end.

My feet and hands were strapped to a special post called the *Bock.* My tormentor brought down the whip with a vengeance. The first four strokes caused grotesque pain but seemed to crush the nerve endings in my buttocks. Though the rest of the blows came with equal violence, I was numb. I counted loudly, "10...15...20...25." And then it was over. I reported, "No. 69733 received 25 strokes for desecrating the bicycle of an SS." My buttocks were mangled. Deep fissures cut my flesh. I could neither sit nor lie on my backside for weeks. But to my relief, my wounds never oozed pus and they eventually healed.

It occurred to me that just as Johe had saved me with the rabbit food, so I could use my position in the mess hall to help a few prisoners. Of course, it was risky. An inmate might accept my help and then turn me in to the SS to get a reward. One day two electricians showed up to make repairs. They wore purple triangles—these were the first Jehovah's Witnesses I had seen in Buna. I rejoiced to know I would be able to give them some leftovers. I could trust them not to betray me. Without exchanging a word with me, they would empty their toolbox and remove the bottom tray. I would pour soup into the empty space underneath. A chronic problem with the electrical installation brought them back often.

This good deed uplifted me and helped me to stifle the extreme repugnance I felt at listening to the vulgar talk of the SS around the tables. Liquor, women, and pornography filled their lives. I could have no visible reaction. Even when I washed blood-stained uniforms, I had to do so mechanically, concealing my profound nausea.

When we were alone, "my" SS man from Mannheim again transgressed the barrier between *Übermensch* and *Untermensch*. He sorely needed a listening ear. Witnessing the defeat of the German army in the east, the landing of the Allies in the west, and the relentless bombing from above, he feared the inevitable future. Again he told me that he was on a runaway train with no way to get off. "When it crashes, I'll die," he said.

> At nightfall, Hitler Youth, *Jungvolk,* and *BDM* [League of
> German Girls], nearly 1,000 boys and girls, marched
> unitedly to the Lorscherweg sports field.
> —*Summer Solstice 1936 in Viernheim*

The guard's Mannheim accent revived my remote memories of Hitler Youth marches in Viernheim. I recalled seeing waves of young men in uniform marching proudly amid a sea of swastika flags. People believed in their legendary ancestors, their invincible heroes. Streets were given new names, to revive the glories of the past. The main road going toward the Felsenmeer had been renamed the Nibelungenstrasse, after Wagner's great opera based on an ancient Germanic poem.

> Our banner flutters before us.
> Our banner represents the new era.
> And our banner leads us to eternity.
> Yes, our banner means more to us than death.
> —*"Hitler Youth Banner Song"*

How long would it be before young and old realized that the Nazi State held them prisoner? Why could they not see that the belligerent and racist rhetoric of the party was leading to a totalitarian state that demanded blind and unconditional submission? Did they not see that the road to Hitler's "greater Germany" would be paved with violence and blood? The responsibility for this travesty lay upon the shoulders of the leading men of the nation who had misled their youth.

The Mannheim SS man sought me out even more frequently as the Soviet army neared Germany. While he watched me clean fresh bloodstains out of his trousers, he unloaded his fears on me. Only alcohol and women helped him to carry on. When the liquor-induced stupor wore off, then this "superman," strong and handsome, collapsed and cried like a child. I pitied this creature who had once been an innocent baby in a cradle and had grown up to be a violent predator. Now he could finally understand what it meant to ponder the future in mortal fear. These glimpses into his inner turmoil reminded me of the intriguing discussions I had had with the purple triangles about the existence of evil.

The explanation, they said, lies right within the Holy Writings, where it describes an unseen spirit who manipulates sinful men, whether wicked or weak. I believed in the Almighty One as a God of justice and mercy who alone could judge these men and their deeds.

Had I not been armed with this knowledge, I would have lost control long before, not so much over my tongue, but over the look of disgust I struggled to hide. Daily in the SS camp, I came face-to-face with the utter depravity of the so-called Master Race, cogs in the hideous machinery of murder. They only knew the order from their superior, who in turn had to execute the order from above. They only marched in time to their orders, trampling humanity in their path. Their strength came from strong liquor. The more they drank, the more vile they became. When their eyes waxed foggy and gray, the threat of bloodlust rose. The majority of SS men in the camp sullied themselves by orgies of unbridled violence.

The recent arrivals brought the news. In broken German they told us about the breakdown of the Third Reich's army, its disintegration at the eastern and the western fronts. Their report stirred a mixture of hope and fear. Rumors swirled among the better informed of a planned mass annihilation of prisoners before the Allies arrived. Deliverance or mass extermination, what choices! As the battle lines approached, we didn't know whether to feel hope or utter despair.

Snow and ice returned. The frigid wind beat our shriveled bodies during the painstaking head counts. This was my sixth winter—would I survive? Nothing had changed in the camp routine. Despite the approaching Allied forces, the work units continued to march out in formation. The *Kapos* still shouted, "left, two, three, four!" Even the marching songs still cut the air. The relentless inspection of our striped uniforms and of our shoes went on as usual. As always, the slightest offense brought severe punishment.

Our thin soup still consisted of rotten vegetables, and the exchange of bread for cigarettes continued to shorten lives. Bread, the most precious and coveted of all goods, was the favored target of thieves. It was never safe, just like our lives. Every day I went to work, along with the men attached to my number. I passed the gate daily with relief, giving the password "No. 69733 plus nine." Dread still hung in the air, and wanton killing continued in the camp. We still stood for unending hours at attention. And then one day during a blinding snowstorm, the order came to evacuate the camp.

8

Block after block of inmates poured out of Buna. In an endless column, the snow-covered prisoners advanced into the falling night. "Faster, you *Schweinehunde*," the SS guards shouted, their fingers ever ready on the trigger. They told us we had to escape the beastlike Russians. "Faster, faster…," they moved us toward an unknown destiny. The guards changed shifts every two hours, but we prisoners couldn't stop. In the pitch darkness of the night, we pushed against the bitter wind that hindered our steps. Prisoners who were slow were trampled by the human wave. Once in a while, the sound of a gunshot told us that someone had given up and sat down on the side of the road.

At last, the order came to stop. In the dim light of the January dawn, we saw the vague outline of a barn. It would shelter us for a few hours of rest. We sank down on the damp straw. The blizzard penetrated the wooden slats. I fought weakly to keep from succumbing to the "white sleep," the soft, cold-induced slumber from which one would not awake. When the order came to resume our march, many lay peaceful and motionless. Some had died from the cold; others had simply surrendered to exhaustion. A shroud of driven snow blew through the cracks and covered them.

We were emaciated, rag-covered silhouettes dragging our aching limbs through the snowdrifts. Our needy stomachs groaned. Our tattered bodies screamed in the cold. Even the SS men seemed weary. They shuffled along and let our march formation dissolve. They no longer drove us, nor did they bark obscenities. They only commanded us to move, to continue toward the unknown destination.

Our legs had no time to recover on the endless, nonstop march. Through the whole night the blizzard raged on, draining our remaining strength. Our bread long gone, we had only snow to eat. How could we endure much longer, and would it be worth the torturous march? To stop, just to sit down in the snow, would have been so easy. We could burrow into it and wait for the soft white sleep. Or if discovered, we could count on a "mercy shot" to put a quick end to the ordeal. When the blizzard, the miles, and the hunger had ground down their will to live, men chose that way out. No one mourned them. Each one wrestled alone with his pain-wracked body. SS guards on motorcycles controlled the human stream. They offered dubious encouragement, saying, "We will soon reach Gleiwitz…just a few more miles."*

How many arrived in Gleiwitz out of all those who left Buna, no one knew. At least I had walked away from Auschwitz-Buna alive. The place of my father's birth, Auschwitz, could easily have become my grave, as it had for countless others. It was already a miracle that I had survived this far and now stood in a field by the railroad track. Surrounded by SS and long deprived of food, we had to jump to keep the blood from freezing in our veins until the train arrived. So Gleiwitz would not be our final destiny either. Our despair stretched on.

The SS man from Mannheim called me. Next to him stood a sack. "Max, in this sack are loaves of bread and sausage. Every SS man gets one of each." The SS men may have been hungry, but I was ravenous. Nevertheless, I did my duty. I waded among the milling crowd, distributing to each SS man one loaf and one sausage. At the end, one portion remained. I had to report to the

---

*Gleiwitz was a subcamp of Auschwitz.

Mannheim SS. In an undertone he said, "Max, make it disappear. The journey will be long, very long." Swiftly, I hid my manna in my trousers and trudged back to join the snow-covered drove of living skeletons who sat huddled on the ground.

The heavy snowfall blanketed the field, merging landscape and horizon in a gray gloom. The twilight brought with it a locomotive, trailed by a string of open coal cars. It screeched to a halt. This could not be meant for us. Even cattle bound for the slaughterhouse would not ride in such cars, exposed to the fury of winter.

But we were less than cattle in the eyes of the SS men who herded us toward the open cars. Climbing up onto the snowy platform, we gave way to panic. All those wretched days we had marched, supposedly to escape the clutches of the Russian Mongolian barbarians. Had it all been a cruel prank? Would it all end here in a morgue on wheels? Again we had been victimized by SS lies.

What was left of our meager hopes deserted us. The train of doom moved out of Gleiwitz. The nightmare resumed. We hadn't eaten for days. Hunger turned some insane and brought others to blows. The silent killer, the white sleep, did the work for the SS and the *Kapos*. For those who survived, the clothes of the dead were a windfall. On the second day, the train stopped. We received the order to step out of the car to receive a bowl of watery soup. We had to move the corpses to another car. Every morning thereafter, two men took the bodies, with their permanently contorted faces, and pitched them into the next car. The cavernous eyes, open mouths, and shrunken forms failed to awaken in us the slightest emotion. We had lived among corpses for years. We lifted our gaze to the gray heavens and thought only of our hunger. Desperation stalked us and took more victims.

Slowly, the train passed through the city of Prague. On the overpasses above the tracks, people looked down and burst out in shrieks of horror. They slapped their heads in disbelief as others came running toward the commotion. Before them lay the macabre vision of an open, rolling grave. Every second car had a growing heap of corpses lying helter-skelter. In the other cars, living skeletons let out anguished screams.

Allied bombing had destroyed tracks and bridges, delaying rail traffic. Every so often, our train had to pull off the track to let the regular train pass. Often the tracks where we waited led off into fields where we would sit for hours under tight SS guard. Fresh waves of fear rippled through the remaining prisoners. Would it be here that we would finally fall prey to their sordid scheme? The snow and frigid wind seemed to whirl right through our empty bellies, taking more lives. We heaved the corpses into the next car and had more room to move about, all in a vain effort to generate some warmth. Again we started off. Despair mounted a fresh assault and tried to wrestle us to the ground one last time. The hope imparted to me by my friends in Neuengamme now amounted to one simple petition: "Into your hands, *O Adonai,* I entrust my life."

9

Buchenwald; January 26, 1945. The train came to a halt. The ex-asperated SS guards shouted, *"Raus!"* In my railcar, only a dozen men had survived. We were ordered to march, but we stumbled like drunken men. We reached an iron gate that carried a stark pronouncement: *"JEDEM DAS SEINE"* (To each what he de-serves). More SS men awaited us. We were to go to the Small Camp, next to the main camp, to an area specially reserved for Jews. The procedure in Buchenwald mirrored that of the other camps. Only this time, the shave and burning disinfectant were somehow welcome. After a shower, we were issued clean clothes. *We had survived.* Now we would have a roof over our heads and hot soup each day. We tasted a certain burst of success—we had survived this far.

We were led to believe that Buchenwald would be better than Auschwitz; we found out soon enough that this was another SS lie. The bunks were overloaded. Once more it was impossible to lie on our backs. In the Small Camp, another efficient killer did its work. Typhus took a heavy toll. Many burned with high fever. Medical care was nonexistent. The sick couldn't so much as lift themselves out of their bunks to go to the latrine. A choking stench filled the air. Our weakened bodies had no resistance left. After our long battle to survive, would it all end in the crematorium here?

An announcement called for volunteers for the daily task of carrying a 50-liter cauldron of hot soup from the main camp kitchen to the Small Camp. At first, I thought I couldn't do it—I felt so weak. Yet, I presented myself and they accepted me. In the back of my mind, I hoped that somewhere in the main camp I would find the purple triangles. Day after day, I dragged the heavy load. I could hardly lift it off the ground. But the dream of finding a way out of this hell gave me strength and helped to blunt the constant fear of typhus.

Weeks slid by while I trudged back and forth carrying the soup cauldron. One day I spotted a purple triangle among the kitchen staff. I managed to meet him. Otto Becker was his name. Could he possibly get me out of the Small Camp? I asked. He knew how dangerous it would be. He told me that he would not attempt it but that he would try to contact a block overseer who came from my home region.

The *Kapo* Kindinger, a Communist from Reichenbach, agreed to ask his overseer for permission to bring me over to his barrack. This overseer, in turn, had to get the approval from the SS. In spite of the drastic quarantine to keep the typhus epidemic con-

---

Otto Becker. He was active in spreading his faith as early as 1924. In that year, 20 people in a small German village were baptized as Jehovah's Witnesses. He traveled in a 70- to 80-kilometer radius, mostly by bicycle, teaching the Bible. In 1933, when the Nazi ban was imposed, Becker continued his activities in secret. For participating in underground religious activities, Becker was eventually arrested and sentenced to one and a half years in prison. After refusing to divulge information during Gestapo interrogation, Becker was sent to a concentration camp.

In Buchenwald, Becker spent three or four months in the punishment battalion, subject to the most crushing work. Thereafter, he served on a construction work *Kommando*. At one point Becker refused to assist in the installation of an anti-aircraft gun in the guard tower. Despite SS threats, Becker held his ground. After eight and a half years in Nazi captivity, Otto Becker returned home.

fined to the Small Camp, the approvals came through for me to enter Kindinger's barrack under the register number 120422. Maybe now I would have a better chance of survival.

Back again in the routine of endless roll calls, I undertook my assigned task at a building site outside the camp, grateful to be away from the typhus epidemic. Among the workers returning in the evening from work was Fritz Heikorn, a Jewish intellectual. Working under the oversight of Hermann Emter, a *Bibelforscher,* he struggled to lay bricks to make a straight wall. Emter proved to be a patient mentor. He protected Fritz from severe punishment by correcting his work. At the same time, Emter shared his faith and hope. Fritz also became my friend.

Here in Buchenwald, the camp commander had scattered the *Bibelforscher* inmates throughout the barracks as a strategy to break up the Witnesses' solidarity. Despite the possibility of severe consequences, Jehovah's Witnesses would talk about their faith and try to encourage others. Out of love for the Holy Writings, they passed separate pages of the Scriptures from one to another. If it were discovered, the worst punishment could be expected.

Fritz Heikorn told me about a Bible discussion he had had with Emter about the coming of the Messiah. The discussion stirred Fritz's determination to put aside his exhaustion and learn more about the Bible. His keen desire to learn awoke my spiritual thirst again.

We both struggled with the question of the Messiah's identity. We were so confused. As Jews, our people had awaited the coming of the Messiah for centuries. The purple triangles seemed so sure of their hope in Jesus as the Messiah and the Savior of mankind. But to us Jews, it seemed the name of Jesus had only brought death and devastation, not salvation. Throughout the ages his followers, from the Crusaders to our churchgoing neighbors, had cruelly spilled our blood. How could he be our Messiah? And yet the purple triangles had explained to us that the teachings of Jesus condemned what people have done to Jews in his name. Moreover, we had seen with our own eyes how these Christians were willing to suffer and die rather than share in harming anyone. They put their full trust in Jesus as the Messiah who would vanquish evil. Could they be right?

How could I presume to contradict the teachings of our fathers, our grandfathers, and our venerable rabbis? Could it really be so that the Messianic Kingdom had drawn near, promising peace, not only for us Jews but for all men of goodwill? Fritz and I became absorbed in searching together for logical proof that the Messianic promises would soon be fulfilled. From the worn-out pages of the Bible shone a beacon of hope we longed to cling to, even as darkness and hopelessness surrounded us.

Kindinger knew that I was in danger of collapsing from hunger. He secretly gave me extra bread. I shared it with Fritz, who was beginning to show the first signs of becoming a *Muselmann*. Together, we each ate a little bite, a lifesaving morsel for us.

I passed my sixth winter in camp. One day Kindinger called me. Privately, he revealed to me that the American army was getting close. He had heard a rumor that the SS had received orders to make sure no prisoners survived. They would carry out the order immediately, he told me, starting with the Jews. We would be taken to the railroad tracks, loaded into cattle cars, and brought to the forest. There we would be forced to dig trenches and then stand at the edge to take an SS bullet. When the next trench was dug, the dirt would cover up the corpses in the first trench. Kindinger made an unbelievable, courageous offer. He would find a way to hide me. I asked him to hide Fritz too. "Impossible," he said. "It's dangerous enough to hide one Jew!"

I couldn't bear to leave Fritz to face death alone. So side by side, we marched to the train tracks as ordered. The tracks terminated near the camp, at the edge of the forest. The SS men were jumpy and drove the prisoners into near hysteria. The prisoners' plaintive cries were heartbreaking. Fritz had a few pages from Revelation, the last book of the Bible. I suggested that we slip behind a woodpile not far from the

When I returned to Buchenwald in 1995, I found the very woodpile we had sat behind

tracks and away from the chaos. There we could draw upon the strength of God's Word to meet our death calmly and with dignity.

From the other side of the woodpile arose the roar of mayhem. The SS screamed, shoving and flailing the frenzied prisoners. The squealing doors slammed shut, and the engine pulled the train out into the woods, leaving us behind. As the sound of the train receded, we sat behind the woodpile paralyzed in disbelief.

We couldn't decide what to do. The sounds of cannon fire and exploding shrapnel heralded the approach of the American army. Should we sit and wait for them, on the chance that we could hide from the SS? At that moment a work unit passed by, dragging back to the camp. Fritz and I looked at each other and decided to join up with them. We would try to make it through the camp gate undetected. As best we could, we covered our yellow prisoner symbols that designated us as Jews and shuddered at the thought of being discovered.

At the entrance of the camp, we passed without being checked. The SS dashed around in total confusion. Amid the chaos the loudspeaker blared, "*Bibelforscher,* assemble in Barrack No. 1." This order sounded to us like a message from heaven.

After our inconceivable escape, we entered Barrack No. 1. The purple triangles let us in without hesitation, even though our tell-tale uniform symbol could have brought calamity on all of them. It was like another world inside. The people looked like they did elsewhere, with dark, sunken eyes and frames covered by paper-thin skin. Yet, they had the same serene bearing as the *Bibelforscher* I had met in Neuengamme four years earlier. During dark years in the pits of inhumanity, their faith and hope had not faded. They seemed to sense impending victory by virtue of their loyalty to God's Word and faith in His salvation.

We exulted over our providential escape. Hermann Emter introduced us to members of the brotherhood; we were welcomed as part of the family. The number of *Bibelforscher* in the barrack gradually swelled to 180.

We did not know whether the SS would carry out their murderous evacuation plan or not. The insecurity of the approaching hours left the group of Witnesses unaffected. Whatever their ultimate fate, they savored the moment of unity. Their quiet composure impressed upon Fritz and me the depth of their reliance on God.

The battlefront drew closer; the bombing grew ever louder. The *Bibelforscher* decided to stay in the barrack to avoid the explosions and the gunfire from both sides. Perhaps the purple triangles also suspected that there would be an uprising by the Communists in the camp. Whatever the reason, they made a wise decision. It seemed like the safest place in the camp to be at that moment.

Fritz and I sat numbly in the barrack, partly from exhaustion and partly from the shock of having come so close to being murdered in the woods. Outside the earth shook from the artillery blasts as showers of shrapnel came ever closer. How easily our wooden barrack could be blown up or burned down, finishing the job for the SS!

Soon we heard the camp break out in tumult. Had the front reached as far as us? Would there be a battle right here in the camp? Tense hours dragged by. Then, a voice over the loudspeaker announced that American soldiers had arrived. Our barrack door flew open. Young American soldiers in military uniforms stood in the doorway. We beheld our liberators, living proof that this was not a dream. We were alive and free—a miracle we could scarcely comprehend.

We heard that many of the first prisoners to crowd around the liberators had suddenly dropped dead. The soldiers, who were extremely shocked at the sight of such great misery, spontaneously started distributing their chocolate rations. But their well-meaning generosity had meant the death of the starving men, whose weakened systems could not tolerate such rich food. Despite the liberation, the camp managed to take yet a few more victims.

Now that the prisoners had been freed, new captives took their place. Though many of the SS had fled, some had been captured. Some among the former prisoners sought vengeance on their oppressors. They tortured and even killed some SS men and *Kapos* while jeering crowds looked on. The impulse to even the score was natural, to be sure, but the purple triangles didn't join in these new "sports."

The ranking U.S. army officers took serious measures to bring some kind of order to the camp. First and foremost, the masses of emaciated people needed immediate care, so that they would have sufficient strength to return to their homelands. The real walk to freedom lay days or weeks away.

The former prisoners continued dwelling in barracks, but the quarters were scrubbed and sanitized. The same kitchen, the same soup cauldron, the same lineup for distribution—but this was a different world! We felt that we were again part of humanity. The cauldron brimmed with a nourishing milk-and-rice gruel. We could have as much as we wanted. But would it be enough? For most of us, our lives still hung by a very thin thread.

We had almost forgotten that a world existed outside the camp until we saw a stream of people pass tentatively through the camp gates. While the camp still reeked amid shriveled corpses and squalor, the American authorities demanded that the local population—who claimed they knew nothing of the existence of the camp—come and see the cruel reality with their own eyes. If the people of the nearby city of Weimar wanted food, they first had to take a walking tour through hell.

In the slow-moving line, I saw people reluctant to look upon the fruitage of the "Third Reich." They covered their grimacing faces with handkerchiefs, not only to wipe away tears but to block the choking stench. As they passed in front of the crematorium, they saw the glassy eyes of naked corpses staring back at them reproachfully. Many of the people vomited or fainted.

Before them lay a powerful lesson about the real face of Nazism, which had long been camouflaged behind the hypnotic marches and highly polished SS. The devastated land, the vanquished military, the severe privation, and now the grotesque scenes of barbarity had ground the German nationalistic pride to dust. Would they realize that their compliance or cowardice had suffocated their consciences and, as a result, reduced Germany to ashes?

On the day of Liberation, the purple triangles gathered and joined in a prayer of thanks to their Savior, Jehovah. One of them, Wilhelm Töllner, quoted many words from the holy men and prophets of old. I remember well the verses: "We became like those who were dreaming," and, "The name of Jehovah is a strong tower." This momentous talk solidified in my heart the determination to show my gratitude for my life. Both Fritz and I vowed to live up to the meaning of the name Jew by openly praising God and becoming Witnesses to his Holy Name.

Now that they were free to move about, the purple triangles —Jehovah's Witnesses—met in the Falkenhaus. In this stone build-

Wilhelm Töllner (1900-1983). Born in Schalkmühle, Westphalia, Germany, Wilhelm Töllner and his wife, Klara, were both imprisoned for possessing and distributing Bible literature. They lost custody of their two children, Ruth and Wilhelm, Jr. A special court in Hannover sentenced Töllner to one year in prison in 1936. In December 1937, he was sent to Buchenwald, where he found 350 Bible Student prisoners, all of whom were assigned to a "punishment block" for four months. Extremely hard labor began with the wake-up call at 4:15 a.m. and ended only at 9:30 p.m. In the summer of 1938, at one work site, the prisoners had no access to drinking water. Some Bible Students obtained permission from the *Kommandant* to run an emergency cable from a transformer to a pumping station. Thereafter, all the prisoners had fresh drinking water. Töllner, an outstanding speaker and a dynamic leader, assumed a leading role among the Bible Student prisoners. He remained in Buchenwald until the end of the war.

ing, Leon Blum, the former premier of France, had been held prisoner. Leon Blum had been freed and had left the camp. A purple triangle had been his orderly, and thus through this privileged prisoner, the Witnesses had access to this house. There in Blum's bathtub Fritz and I were baptized by the Witnesses. Our complete immersion symbolized our vow to dedicate ourselves to God and to his work. From this place, some Witnesses who had enough strength walked down to Weimar, where they visited homes urging people to take the Bible in hand and to live by it.

Hope and faith now prevailed, but our bodies remained extremely weak. A medical examination revealed the reason—a rheumatoid infection. Fritz and I both ended up in the infirmary. The luxury of lying in a bed with white sheets was lost on me. I burned with fever and eventually lost consciousness—it must have been for two weeks. I waged my last battle in the camp against death.

The rheumatoid infection would scar my heart permanently. Slowly, though, I could feel myself getting stronger.

Finally, the army doctor gave me permission to leave the infirmary. The devoted care of the medical staff had literally put me back on my own two feet. My heartbeat quickened at the thought of crossing the dense green forest surrounding the camp. At one time it had been an impenetrable no-man's-land, where SS men and dogs patrolled constantly. Now the place was filled only with the fresh green scent of spring.

It seemed unbelievable—yet it was true—the time had come to pick up our lives. We had to keep telling ourselves that it wasn't a dream. As the group of Witnesses dispersed, we bid one another an emotional farewell. Among those departing was Fritz Adler, a veteran of the camp who had performed our baptism in Leon Blum's bathtub. He eventually reached Magdeburg in East Germany, where the German headquarters of the Witnesses had been located before 1933. The Russian army now controlled this zone.

A Witness from Rhineland managed to obtain a truck, and I left with him. Sitting on the platform of the flatbed truck didn't make for easy travel. The roads and bridges still carried the ravages of repeated bombings. Several times we had to reroute because the way became impassable. We drove through the remains of bombed-out cities gaily adorned with blossoming apple trees. The ruined panorama dampened our mood and brought up the question each one dreaded to ponder, *Who will be waiting for me at home?*

Friedrich Adler (1889-1970). Friedrich ("Fritz") Adler was born in Lugau, in the district of Chemnitz, Germany. He worked at the post office until 1925, when he became a full-time Bible Student "pilgrim," or traveling minister. In 1935, Adler was arrested. A special court in Halle sentenced him to one year and six months. After his release, he resumed his religious activity, for which he went to prison again several times. Finally, prison authorities turned Adler over to the Gestapo, who sent him to Buchenwald concentration camp and gave him prisoner number 1808.

Adler served as the secretary for the camp's first *Kommandant,* Arthur Rödl. In this position, he found ways to help fellow prisoners, including some of the several hundred purple triangles in the camp. After five years of postwar freedom, from 1945 to 1950, Adler was arrested by the Stasi (East German secret police) on charges of espionage and sentenced to life imprisonment. The sentence was later reduced to 15 years, most of which he spent in solitary confinement in Brandenburg. He was released in August of 1964 and moved to West Germany. He died on December 2, 1970, and was buried in Wiesbaden. Adler spent a total of 9 years in Nazi prisons and camps and 15 years imprisoned in East Germany.

10

I didn't expect that any of my immediate family would be waiting at home for me. My father was dead; my mother and sisters were an ocean away. I reached Viernheim, nestled as before in the asparagus fields. The Oppenheimers' house was intact, but much of the city lay in ruins. The mayor seemed chagrined to see me. He could not offer me a place to stay in the bombed-out city. But he did give me a motorbike that had belonged to an SA man killed during the war. The tattoo on my forearm proved useful. By showing my bluish number and my liberation certificate from Buchenwald, I could get gasoline at any Allied gas depot.

From Viernheim I decided to go to Reichenbach. There, I recognized some of the children, now grown-up. Nothing had changed in the old neighborhood—or almost nothing. My family's tiny home was now occupied by a humble family. I could not bring myself to have them evicted.

So I went to the mayor to ask for shelter. Like the mayor of Viernheim, he seemed embarrassed and reluctant to help me find lodging. I insisted that, since Reichenbach had not been bombed, there must be a place I could live. He was obliged to help me, though he only did so out of duty. He finally told me where to look for lodging. My return to Reichenbach was bittersweet as I realized that, for various reasons, not everyone welcomed my sur-

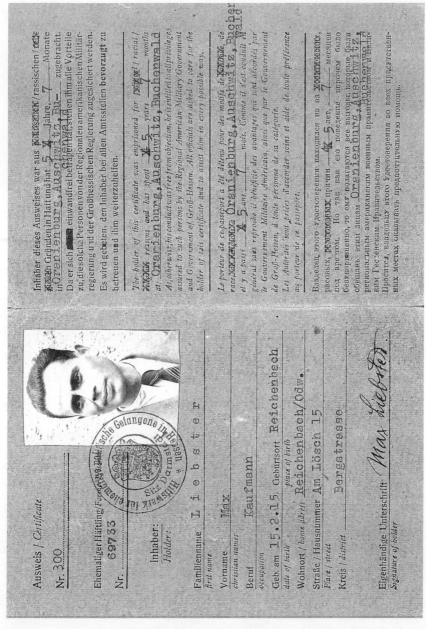

My liberation certificate

vival—in some, antisemitism was still deep; others had taken the property of Jews; still others were uncomfortable because of their guilty consciences.

The ramshackle house to which the mayor sent me looked more like a depot than a home. Frau Hochgenug, the elderly owner, didn't live alone—a swarm of cats occupied whatever space they could find, between pots and pans and fur-covered furniture. Her cooking was most primitive, but this 80-year-old woman loved to listen as I read the Bible aloud. I took up residence there in a small room.

I put forth a great effort to resume normal life. But six years of marching to the orders of the SS had turned me into a mechanical man. Anything I did on my own took infinitely longer than it had before I was arrested. I often sat paralyzed, as if I were held in a steel web. When I heard a German shepherd bark, I jumped like a hunted animal. A sound, a smell, or a word would bring visions of horror and destruction flooding back to my eyes. At any instant, I would find myself back in the camp, surrounded by all its suffocating terrors.

To make a living, I visited the wholesalers that the Oppenheimers used to frequent. The merchants were startled and decidedly uneasy at seeing me. But they willingly sold me merchandise to help me get started making a living. I had no grandiose plans. I only wanted to care for my elementary needs.

The people of the Lauter Valley were also shocked to see the *Judemäx'che* (Max the Jew). The news spread like wildfire. I made it my goal to visit every

Working as a salesman, 1946

home to share with them the hope that had helped me survive six years in the camps. Some of the residents expressed genuine relief at my return and gave me a heartfelt welcome.

Others barely hid their deep resentment. They made it clear that they would have preferred that I had vanished. Did they see in my emaciated face the mirror of their own consciences? Yet, I had not come to accuse anyone or to recover what I had lost. Nor did I seek revenge. I would leave that in God's hands.

The war had left the valley itself unscathed. But each home bore battle scars of a different sort. Every family had suffered loss —their men killed, wounded, or missing—and all for nothing, as they now knew. My heart went out to these people who had once been my neighbors. How they had been deceived by a false Messiah! Now he was gone, and they were left bereaved, disillusioned, and poor.

I understood how it felt to be swallowed by darkness. People had disappointed me too. The vicious destruction of the Oppenheimer Brothers store still left a vivid image in my mind. But the sting of betrayal by our "loyal" customers had long since left me, and a sense of pity had taken its place. I thought of the SS guard from nearby Mannheim and wondered about his final fate. What these people needed was hope, like the consolation I had found when I was chained to a man who had lost everything but his faith in God. The purple triangles kept appearing in my life, like the revolving beam of a lighthouse. The powerful beacon had pulled me back from the abyss time and again.

Travel by motorcycle was difficult. But the rain, the cold, and poor roads did not discourage me from looking for my fellow survivors. My first stop was Pforzheim, where I hoped to find the purple triangle with whom I had left the camp. As I came over the mountain, I saw what used to be the city stretched out in a heap of rubble. What about the purple triangle? To my great surprise, I found him in his greenhouse, which was one of the few structures in town that had survived.

Hermann Emter (1904-1990). Karl Hermann Emter, of Freiburg, was baptized as a Bible Student in 1926. The Gestapo arrested Emter in 1936 and sent him to prison in Freiburg. He was assigned to paint 750 prison cell doors, and he used the opportunity to talk about his faith to the prisoners for about one hour each. After completing a two-year prison term, Emter was sent to Dachau and then to Mauthausen. There he saw a fellow Witness tortured to death for refusing to sign a draft document.

Meanwhile, on January 29, 1940, Emter's wife, Elisabeth, was arrested and taken to Ravensbrück concentration camp, leaving their six small children behind. She was killed with other female Witnesses in July of 1942.

After Emter's return to Dachau in the spring of 1940, the SS decided that he was responsible for hindering other Witnesses from renouncing their faith. The guards severed Emter's fingertips with pliers and slated him for execution. The camp typist saved Emter by having him transported to Flossenbürg concentration camp. Emter's continued refusal to do military service brought more severe treatment and another threat of execution.

Hermann Emter was transported from Flossenbürg to Buchenwald and then to the subcamp Ohrdruf. In response to the Allied advance, Emter was sent on an 80-kilometer-long "death march" back to Buchenwald. He gained his freedom on April 12, 1945.

From there I traveled south to Freiburg to see Hermann Emter. He had started a construction business, and to my delight, Fritz Heikorn was staying with him. Like me, Fritz had found no survivors of his family at home. Emter and I traveled to Karlsruhe to visit Willi Johe, the rabbit keeper to whom I owed my life. I was one of the few with a means of transportation. But a motorcycle is no way to travel during the wet season. I went to the county officials in Hesse and asked them if I could obtain a car. They gave me a letter and the address of a former Nazi who had been barred from holding a driver's license. I was able to buy his car for a cheap price, which made things much easier.

Willi Johe (1898-1962). Born in Rastatt, Germany, Willi Johe served in the German army in World War I at age 18. Before an assault on French forces, the army chaplain blessed the soldiers' rifles. The ensuing bloodbath caused Johe to ponder the sense-lessness of war against "enemies" who, like him, had been drafted to fight the war. After his discharge, he became a Bible Student.

Johe, with his wife and two sons, lived in his newly built home in Karlsruhe until the Nazis evicted them for not voting in the Nazi-controlled elections. The family had to move into a bar-rack for the poor. Their life among the marginalized made it easy for the Gestapo to monitor Johe's activities. In 1937, two Gestapo agents searched their quarters for Bible literature. Al-though they found nothing, they arrested Johe and took him to a court in Mannheim. He received a two-year prison sentence, which he served in Freiburg.

On the day of his release, the authorities presented Johe with a declaration renouncing his faith and pledging his allegiance to Hitler. When Johe refused to sign the document, he was sent to Sachsenhausen concentration camp. From there he went to Neuengamme concentration camp, where he suffered tortures specially reserved for Jehovah's Witnesses. After he again refused to sign the declaration of renunciation, he received 25 strokes with a leather-covered steel whip. Two more refusals brought him the same punishment, for a total of 75 strokes that one day.

As the war drew to a close, Johe and other inmates of Wilhelmshaven (a subcamp of Neuengamme) had to board a ship destined to be sunk in the Baltic Sea. When the ship hit a sandbar, Allied forces captured it and brought the prisoners safely to Flensburg.

Johe's wife had been arrested in 1944, but the whole family was reunited after the war. Johe found a family with eight children living in his house, and he decided not to evict them. He died at age 64, the result of the physical abuse inflicted during his incarceration.

As I traveled through the devastated land, I could see how people suffered. Displaced people huddled together in barely hab-itable ruins, often far away from their home regions. The sense of hopelessness and dislocation did not seem to abate over time. Germany was now divided into four sectors: the American, British, and French sectors, where communication was possible, and the Russian sector, which was under strict control.

I became the liaison for the Witnesses between Lörrach, a city on the Swiss border, and Wiesbaden, where they set up a small office. Erich Frost and Konrad Franke ran the office, which coordinated the congregations of Jehovah's Witnesses in the country. Both Frost and Franke had been hunted down by the Gestapo because of their secret religious activities. Both had survived years in the camps. The Wiesbaden office became a true haven for me. And Franke's wife was a wonderful cook. She also darned my socks and did my laundry.

Now, with the help of Witnesses in Switzerland and the relief supplies coming from the Watch Tower Society in America, the local Witnesses began to recover from the brutal persecution and rebuild their lives. They also set about reorganizing the witnessing work in Germany. As the liaison, I picked up Bible literature at the Swiss border and brought it to the small groups of Witnesses in various cities and towns. I found it a challenge to navigate the bombed-out streets. Once, my motorcycle hit a deep pothole, sending me and all my booklets swimming in mud.

In my valley a small group gathered to study the Bible together. They wanted to attend a convention that the Witnesses were holding in Nuremberg—on the very grounds where Nazi battalions had celebrated their impending world conquest. But travel was still extremely difficult. So I hitched an open wagon to my car and brought nine friends along to the convention. Some 6,000 Witnesses assembled under a huge tent at the Zeppelin Meadow. They listened in astonishment to the experiences of the survivors. While the Witnesses worshiped their God on the former Nazi parade grounds, Nazi perpetrators in another part of Nuremberg were being tried and condemned. The verdicts were read the very day our convention concluded.

Ida, my sister, managed to send word to me from America. I learned that she had already applied for a visa for me before the war. This visa was still valid. But her offer created a dilemma. I felt I had finally found my place and was accomplishing much good, comforting the local people and helping Witnesses in various congregations. Frost and Franke, however, encouraged me to take advantage of the opportunity to go to America. So I gave them my car and my motorcycle and headed off to a new life.

11

The possibility of leaving the war-ravaged continent was a golden opportunity. For Nazi victims, especially Jewish survivors, it offered a new lease on life and a recovery of our dignity. Nevertheless, it meant leaving much behind: our homes, our dear friends, and the graves of our ancestors. The farewells were heartrending and tearful. We boarded the *USS Ernie Pyle* on a gray and misty day in Bremerhaven in late December 1946. The chilly air sent shivers through us and silenced the nervous chatter.

All the males slept in quarters usually occupied by GIs, one man to a hammock. The quarters were so cramped that when a man sat in his hammock, he would rest on the stomach of the man lying beneath him.

We settled ourselves as best we could for the seven-day westbound voyage. Only the children seemed excited. Other passengers fidgeted uncomfortably, especially those from Central Europe who had never seen the ocean before. We felt the constant roll and forward movement of the ship as it threaded its way through the once mine-infested channel between the Continent and England. The foghorn wailed mournfully as we headed toward the open sea.

We were all Jews on board, and among the passengers were many camp survivors. Some of them aimed to make a brilliant success of themselves in the New World. But they had carried the stigma of their Jewishness through the long years of Nazi rule and had suffered unspeakable abuses. Such scars are not so easily erased. Moreover, though we could give one another some emotional support, to a certain extent, these were burdens we had to bear alone. Who else could *really* understand what each of us had been through? I looked around at their faces and could pick out those still broken and afflicted. They sat in silence, staring with vacant eyes. Others burned with an insatiable desire for revenge and vowed not to rest until retribution had been attained.

We all needed to go through a healing process, to regain self-esteem and self-confidence, and to rise above the past. The climb out of the abyss and into a normal life would be long and hard, especially for those of us tormented by memories that defied human language to describe. The anguish locked inside each survivor of Nazi terror would require decades to fade away, if ever it could.

How my heart went out to these tormented souls! I wanted to lighten their burdens, just as someone had reached out to me again and again at the very moments when I thought I could not endure any longer.

I found many listening ears among the men who, like me, preferred to stay on deck. We savored the fresh, salty air and the rhythm of the waves slapping the ship. We talked of hopes and dreams and passages from the Scriptures that soothed our sorrows. For me, the Messianic rule had become a reality, the true and only hope for mankind. Only the Messiah could bring harmony to this turbulent world.

At times, the conversation would drift toward our painful pasts. No one could bear to speak about the subject in great detail. I felt compelled to tell my companions about the phenomenon I had seen in the very bowels of the camps—a group of men who dared to resist the madman Hitler and his hateful ideology. No one I talked to had had personal contact with the purple triangles, but they were fascinated to hear that Jehovah's Witnesses, mostly Germans, had refused to *Heil Hitler* and to serve in his army. The fact that the Witnesses were a Christian group made it all the more curious. It was not lost on any Jew that the majority of our church-going neighbors, respectable "Christians," had cheered the Führer enthusiastically.

My eyes welled up with tears as I told them about the *Bibelforscher* barrack in Neuengamme. Those listening could scarcely believe it when I related how the purple triangles cared for one another and welcomed us Jews, extending to us the dignity that the Nazis had long since stripped away. I told them that the Witnesses even risked severe punishment to help us and give us food.

Of course, it sounded like a myth that Witnesses could walk out of the camps if they would sign a declaration renouncing their faith. No one could fathom that the Nazis would let anyone go free for a simple signature. But it was true. August Dickmann would not have faced the firing squad had he signed the paper and taken up arms for Germany. Other Witnesses I knew had gone through SS torture sessions to try to make them change their minds—but few did.

After six years in five camps, I had seen the effects of the Nazi dehumanization program. I had encountered both civilized men who turned into worse than animals and ordinary men who had become heroes. It was clear to me that their faith in the Messianic promises had sustained the Witnesses in their fierce loyalty to God. I had seen it with my own eyes. It seemed altogether right for me to witness about the Witnesses. I felt it my duty.

Listening to my account, many were greatly surprised. Others were skeptical and quarreled with me. It was hard for me to understand that talk about faith in God was just too much for some who had been so terribly wounded by men. A young Jew named Hugo Holzmann came over to observe a dispute. From then on, he often sought out my company to engage me in conversation. About this time, the sea began to stir, and the breaks in the clouds disappeared. The breeze picked up and turned into a steady, brisk wind. Soon seasickness overtook most of us. On deck, a group of men became so annoyed with my talk about faith that one man rudely grabbed my Bible and flung it into the foaming ocean, depriving me of my greatest treasure.

This display of bitterness made me sick. We Jews, of all people, had tasted of the violence inflicted by those intoxicated with the bitter potion of intolerance. On board were Jews who had themselves suffered grievously from the destructive power of intolerance. We knew how it had begun: first, by the burning of "un-German" books; then, by spreading propaganda about the so-called enemies of the State; and finally, by physically annihilating these enemies. How sad to see the seeds of intolerance among those who had so recently been victims themselves! But before long, any scornful remarks were drowned out by the howling wind.

The gusts increased in power, and the sea turned leaden gray, tossing foaming whitecaps and spray into the air. A few sunbeams stabbed the angry sky, only to be overwhelmed by an invasion of threatening clouds. One by one, the men took shelter in the hold below, leaving Hugo and me behind on deck.

We found a place where we could watch the prow leap up and down as it fought the huge waves. I tried to match the rhythm of the rocking motion, using my knees and toes like springs. By doing so I staved off the seasickness that had sent most of the men to their hammocks.

After seven days—we had expected to arrive in New York after a week's journey—we still found ourselves in the middle of the Atlantic Ocean. Had the boat taken a detour in search of better weather, or were we just going around in circles? Finally, the wind died down, and the raging sea became calm.

The brief respite only teased us. The storm winds began to build with renewed fury. People gave way to muted panic. Why did the storm return? Could it be a sign of God's wrath? Did the force of evil follow us? Had we escaped destruction in the camps only to fall prey to another relentless foe? Grandiose plans and great expectations dissolved into fear.

For days and nights, the winds and waves seized the boat as if it were held in the jaws of a wild animal shaking it with all its might. The deck was constantly awash as the railing dipped far into the water. The sea swelled upward to form a towering wall high overhead. It was awe inspiring. I watched with frightened fascination as our boat repeatedly dropped into a yawning valley and then miraculously reappeared.

The relentless assault of hail and rain went on and on. An ocean on the rampage seemed determined to shatter us to pieces. As the days passed, we began to doubt the ability of the steamer to withstand the constant pummeling. What chance did we have to come through this alive?

It was only on the 13th day of our journey that the savage attack showed signs of abating. A tempestuous ocean, after battering us mercilessly, finally seemed to be giving up. The wind diminished, the waves died down, and the sun made a brief appearance. Then we plunged into deep fog. The echo of the lapping waves replaced the roar of the churning sea.

The plaintive sound of the foghorn announced our arrival in New York Harbor. Ahead of our steamer, a shadowy figure loomed against the skyline. "It's the gracious lady," someone said, "the Statue of Liberty!" *America.* The news spread like wildfire, echoed from deck to deck, and revived exhausted refugees by the hundreds.

Barely recovered from our harrowing journey, we had to prepare for landing. The biggest challenges lay ahead. We were newcomers in a foreign land, with a new tongue and new customs to learn.

Hundreds of white handkerchiefs waved excitedly in welcome. Absolutely exhausted, we disembarked unsteadily after our 14-day ordeal, only to face the meticulous immigration process. We were drained but greatly relieved to stand on solid ground. I spotted my sister jumping up and down with glee. I had last seen Ida in 1938, but she had hardly changed. Now, nine years later, she was among the high-spirited crowd that had waited seven extra days for our arrival. She waved a handkerchief and called out my name.

Ida hugged me again and again. "My brother, my brother!" I stood there stunned, unable to respond. Next to my elated sister stood Julius Oppenheimer. The last time I had seen him was at the Oppenheimers' departure after "Crystal Night" when they were forced to leave me behind to face the Nazi beast alone. We went to Julius's apartment in Brooklyn. Hugo Oppenheimer and his family came along. We would have a welcome dinner. On the way, I craned my neck to see the towering ships at the piers in midtown New York and the great skyscrapers above my head. It seemed like a dream world.

The tragic news about most of our family put a damper on the euphoria of our reunion. It was good to hear that our sister, Hanna, had made it safely to Argentina. She now lived on an isolated farm and was raising five children. She had worked hard to pay off the debt for the cows that had been provided by a Jewish refugee organization. It was sad to hear that her husband, Adolf, didn't help her carry the load. But Hanna had married Adolf, then a stranger, with the hope that she could save us all. Perhaps we'll never know why only Mum could escape, but at least she was there to help Hanna look after the children.

Settchen, our dear, sickly aunt, had disappeared. Only many years later did we find out what had happened to her. After Mum left for Argentina, Aunt Settchen had been forced to go to an old-age home. At the time, the authorities told my family she died a natural death. The truth came out later, however. She had fallen victim to the Nazi "euthanasia" program.

Of the Liebster family from Aschaffenburg, only my cousins Max and Ilse survived. Uncle Nathan, his wife, and their smaller children could not be saved by friendly neighbors. They

My mother, Bertha Liebster, in Argentina , post-1945

vanished without a trace, swept away by the "final solution."

My uncle Adolf Oppenheimer died shortly before "Crystal Night." His widow (I no longer can remember her name) was sent to the East, never to return. Of my uncles, the only one who managed to escape was Leopold, who worked as a tailor in Stuttgart. Because he had married an "Aryan" and was raising his children in the Protestant faith, he had been overlooked by the Nazi hunters. Fortunately, the people who knew his Jewish background were not Nazi collaborators.

Unlike many of the passengers who had arrived on the *USS Ernie Pyle,* I knew that most of the details of my new life were already settled. My sister, who had paid the Jewish organization that sponsored us, had obtained the needed affidavit from Mr. Sloan. He owned a clothing business in Dunbar, West Virginia, near Charleston. Ida's husband, Sydney, had worked at Sloan's after his arrival from Germany, but he later started a window frame business and was doing very well. Ida had also received her affidavit from Mr. Sloan. She presently worked as a cook in his house. So my accommodations at my sister's house and my job as a window dresser at Sloan's were all set. More than that, my brother-in-law Sydney planned to make me his business partner.

Before leaving New York for Charleston, I asked to visit the central offices of Jehovah's Witnesses. Their headquarters and the printery for the Watch Tower Bible and Tract Society are situated right near the foot of the famous Brooklyn Bridge. Julius took me by subway to the place the Witnesses call *Bethel,* a Hebrew word meaning "House of God."

Charles Eicher, my German interpreter and enthusiastic guide, welcomed me warmly and showed me around. On the eighth floor of the factory, I stood in front of a banner with the colorful inscription: 'This good news of the kingdom will be preached all over the world.' (Matthew 24:14) Those words matched my heart's desire. With excitement, I watched the high-speed printing presses operated by clean-cut young men who were all volunteers. I decided that this was the place for me, and so I turned in an application that day. I was anxious to lend a hand and work among these dedicated people. But first, I was told, I had to learn English.

Once established at Ida and Sydney's place in Dunbar, I met a retired schoolteacher who patiently helped me to master the language. She had me write ten new words every day on a paper folded lengthwise, English on one side and German on the other. Frequently during the day I would pull out the paper and repeat the ten words. Then I would use the new expressions in my conversations.

Despite the language barrier, I quickly became acquainted with the friendly people of the local congregation of Jehovah's Witnesses. I spent many hours going from door to door, speaking about the Bible in my broken English. Mr. Hall, a kindly watchmaker, and other congregation members sometimes came along and gave me much encouragement, even though I'm sure they had a hard time understanding me. Even Sydney's dog, Bush, went with me from door to door, waiting patiently for me outside the homes I visited.

I worked two evenings a week at Sloan's, setting up the window displays. I also had another job Sydney had got for me at a

Jewish club, serving drinks for a few pennies a day. I just scraped by financially.

Sydney assumed I would readily join him in his new business venture selling stainless-steel window and door frames. But I felt a certain obligation to Mr. Sloan, my sponsor, and I knew I would never be able to devote myself to the door and window frame business the way Sydney would expect. I had no idea that Sydney had been anxiously awaiting my arrival and had counted on my help in his venture. He was bitterly disappointed that I didn't choose to accept his generous offer, and he rarely missed an opportunity to show it.

My decision to be one of Jehovah's Witnesses also became an issue. Ida criticized me sharply for spending so much time reading and teaching the Bible when I could have been making a career for myself. She told me how foolish I was and how humiliating it was for them to be feeding a man who had absolutely no ambition. The rabbi tried to mollify her by reminding her she should be grateful that I was alive.

I concluded that life with Ida and Sydney would not be happy for any of us. Sydney was not a man to bend, and I had made a solemn dedication to witness about the Word of God, which I was determined to live by. Matters finally came to a head, and I made preparations to move out. But before I could complete all the arrangements, I woke up one day to find myself inexplicably at the Halls' house. They had to explain to me what had happened.

I had been absent from Bible class one day, and the Halls came over to Ida's to see if I was all right. Ida and Sydney were gone and the house looked all closed up. But the Halls were worried about me and decided they had better check further. They forced open the back door and came up to my attic room. There they found me, unconscious and stricken with a high fever. Brother Hall wrapped me in a blanket and carried me out. The doctor gave a grave diagnosis: I had double pneumonia. He came to the Halls' twice a day for two weeks, and I finally recovered. I was grateful for the Halls' devotion and their gracious invitation to stay with them, but I wanted to live on my own. I ended up in a leaky trailer in their backyard. When it rained, my shoes would swim out the door on their own! It didn't matter, though, because the burning sun dried everything out very quickly.

The Halls had scraped together enough savings to attend a large convention of the Witnesses that was to be held in Los Angeles on August 13–17, 1947. They surprised me with an invitation to travel with them cross-country by car. We had an unforgettable drive across the Great Plains to California, where 30,000 Witnesses gathered. Maxwell Friend, a Swiss Jew, gave one of the lectures. He was a forceful speaker, formerly a dramatic actor and at that time an instructor at the Watchtower Bible School of Gilead in South Lansing, New York. He included me on the program, believing that my experience in the camps could impart profound moral instruction. He helped me prepare my text. After eight months my English was still too limited. This experience built my confidence. I saw that I could use the account of my life to strengthen others in their trials.

12

After waiting for 18 months, I finally received my invitation to go to New York to serve at Bethel. Reflecting back, I am grateful that my German friends Erich Frost and Konrad Franke encouraged me to emigrate to America. Learning English in a land of freedom could open doors to opportunities of all kinds. To be sure, I could have stayed in Dunbar and enjoyed a comfortable life. But I had decided that I should follow my dream to go to Bethel. When I left West Virginia for New York to take up my new assignment as a staff member of Brooklyn Bethel, my sister was genuinely happy for me. Thereafter, we spent vacation time together.

I faced a new career—learning to operate a Linotype machine and typeset foreign languages. It was a great challenge, but a fulfilling one. As part of the close-knit "Bethel family" of more than two hundred volunteers,[*] I thrived on precious friendships with devoted men and women who enriched my life. Seven years passed by like a day. Then I was blessed with Simone, my "Rachel."[**]

I first met Simone Arnold in 1950. My good friend Charles (Charlie) Eicher, who had been my guide on my first visit to Bethel, was very fond of this lovely and serious young lady who had come from his hometown of Mulhouse in Alsace, France. Charlie took

[*]   Like all the other volunteers, I received room and board and a small stipend.
[**] Rachel was the beloved wife of Jacob, the patriarch of the nation of Israel.

My Linotype station at Bethel, 1948–1955

Simone and me to visit one of his German friends. At the time, neither she nor I realized that this was the beginning of a momentous change in our lives.

Charlie told me that Simone and her parents, faithful Witnesses, had been victims of the Nazis. But she had blocked out the pain of her past and distanced herself from anyone who might revive the traumatic memories. We spoke politely in English — after all that she had been through, she was reluctant to speak German, and I couldn't speak French. Our contact was short-lived. The next time I saw her, her attitude hadn't changed. She was completely absorbed in her goal to attend Gilead School and become a Bible teacher in a foreign land.

She came my way again, as lively and charming as ever, in 1953. We both attended a Witness convention at Yankee Stadium, but I got to spend only minutes talking with her. She remained unmoved. I dreamed of her, yet her poise and distance told me that my chances were nil. I was sure that one of the other suitors around her would win her hand. Meanwhile, she graduated from Gilead and went off to Africa.

Simone Arnold, c. 1953

In 1955, I returned to Europe to attend a series of Witness conventions and to see my German friends again. Paris was my first stop. Simone had returned to France and was living and teaching in Paris. At age 25, she was a gracious lady, still single. But something had changed. She agreed to take a walk with me and talk. It was the first time we had spoken candidly.

Immediately, we established a bond of understanding, the kind only survivors can share. I felt even more drawn to Simone, but I sensed her surprise when she learned I was over 40 years old. I traveled on to a second convention, in Nuremberg. As chance would have it, Simone and her parents were there. We sat together during that week. At once, I could see she had overcome her fear that a relationship with me would open a door to the past, a fear that had moved her for more than five years to keep her love for me concealed. We realized that our common sufferings could give us the strength to move on and share a harmonious marriage. We began courting in Nuremberg.

Four months later, in December 1955, I informed the president of the Watch Tower Society, N.H. Knorr, that I would be getting married. I looked forward to attending the 27th class of Gilead School beginning in February 1956. Yet, I left Bethel in February 1956 with a heavy heart. It had been my entire life for nearly seven years.

September 1956. Now I was a married man. Great challenges lay ahead: a new country, a new language, and a wife.

In Paris we lived in a tiny room in an old stone house. My lovely and resourceful Simone turned the place into a tidy, com-

Simone turned our little apartment into a cozy haven

fortable haven. I attended French classes at the *Alliance Française* and worked mornings on the Linotype machine at the Paris office of the Watch Tower Society. Six years elapsed. Then we took on another responsibility. Simone's aged parents needed our support and care. We moved together to a scenic area in the Savoy region of the French Alps. I considered it a great privilege to render help, not only because Adolphe and Emma Arnold had done such an excellent job raising my wonderful wife but also

Simone and Max the day after their wedding

Emma and Adolphe Arnold

The Arnold Family. Simone Arnold and her parents, Adolphe and Emma, suffered severely for adhering to their faith during the Nazi era. They lived in Alsace, France, a disputed region that had alternately been controlled by France and then Germany. The Arnolds became Jehovah's Witnesses a few years before the German invasion of France. The Nazi persecution of the Witnesses began immediately. The regime quickly imposed social and political measures to "Germanize" the region. Consequently, the Witnesses faced mounting pressure to conform. The Arnolds practiced their faith in secret and assisted in the underground distribution of Bible literature.

Adolphe Arnold, an artist, was arrested by the Gestapo in September 1941. He was 44. He was sent to prison and then to several concentration camps: Schirmeck (France), Dachau (Germany), Mauthausen (Austria), and Ebensee (Austria). In Dachau, Adolphe was ordered to paint dolls on ammunition crates in order to disguise them. When he refused to tell "a lie with a paintbrush," As punishment, Nazi doctors performed six weeks of medical experiments on him. One day Adolphe stumbled and fell. An SS guard dealt him a crushing blow to the head with his boot. Adolphe lost his hearing as a result. Another time, an SS doctor knocked out Adolphe's front teeth. The SS repeatedly offered Adolphe the opportunity to sign the declaration renouncing his faith, which he steadfastly refused to do.

When the Gestapo had first arrested Adolphe, they threatened to return and arrest his wife and daughter. Nearly two years later, Emma Arnold, age 45, was arrested and sent to two camps in France: Schirmeck and Gaggenau. Upon her arrival in Schirmeck, Emma refused to mend a military jacket because she did not want to aid the war effort. This act of defiance earned her several months in solitary confinement. Later, she had to live in a barrack with women infected

(continued)

with syphilis. Although near starvation, Emma continued to give moral support and share her faith with other prisoners, including a female member of the French Resistance who was near collapse. The woman, a high-ranking official of the French Red Cross, later credited Emma with saving her life. Emma Arnold was released in April 1945.

Simone Arnold faced severe pressure in school when she refused to give the *Heil Hitler* salute and to sort materials for the war effort. One day a teacher beat her unconscious because she would not support the Nazi program. In 1943, at age 12, she was arrested and sentenced to a penitentiary home in Constance, Germany. There, she was forbidden to talk and was forced to do hard physical labor. The children were only permitted to bathe and to wash their hair once a year. For nearly two years, she endured the constant threat of arbitrary punishments and the harshness of the matrons. If the war had not ended, she would have faced the prospect of transfer to a concentration camp. Emma Arnold arrived at the penitentiary home in late April 1945 and secured the release of her daughter. (Simone tells her own story in the book *Facing the Lion.*)

After they were reunited, the Arnold family resumed their religious activities together and started to rebuild their lives. The physical and emotional toll of the persecution took several years to overcome, but gradually the nightmares and anxieties dissipated. Simone Arnold met Max Liebster in 1950 in New York. Six years later, they were married. For nearly 50 years, they have lived in France and have devoted their lives to each other and to the work they love.

because they had courageously borne the purple triangle in the camps. We nurtured Simone's beloved parents and aunt for the next 27 years.

My devoted Simone has also patiently looked after me, as the ravages of the camps began to take their toll on my health. Nightmares and epileptic seizures disrupted ever so many nights. Even though decades have gone by, we still at times sorely need emotional support from each other to cope with the wounds of the past. I'm quite sure I would not be approaching my tenth decade of life had it not been for the special love and care of my dear companion.

Max and Simone

In the late 1980's, Simone was invited to become a founding member of the *Cercle Européen des Témoins de Jéhovah Anciens Déportés et Internés* (CETJAD, European Circle of Formerly Deported and Interned Jehovah's Witnesses)— an association established to keep the memory of the Jehovah's Witness survivors alive. In the early 1990's, the CETJAD began preparing an exhibition for the 50th anniversary of Liberation. Beginning in Strasbourg, France, Simone and I traveled with an international group of survivors to concentration camp memorials, such as those at Dachau and Ravensbrück. On that trip, I returned to Buchenwald and Sachsenhausen for the first time since the war. We had warm spring weather, but I shivered from the shock of standing in those places again. A few weeks later, I had a heart attack, likely a result of the emotional trauma. Despite it all, I was able to attend a commemorative program in September 1995 at the United States Holocaust Memorial Museum, which bears the motto: "For the dead and the living we must bear witness." This motto resonated strongly with my conscience.

So at age 80, inspired by the CETJAD and by the desire to "bear witness," I began to travel to many lands to share my story. With the generation of survivors dwindling, I am more determined than ever to embed the events of history in the written word and human hearts so that these memories cannot be diminished or erased.

The murder of millions of Jews cannot be forgotten. I will not permit the voices of those who would deny or rewrite the past to win out. The story of the purple triangles must also be told so that it may sustain and strengthen those who face desperate situations of their own.

May others take courage in the knowledge that
hope can conquer despair.

EPILOGUE

The following biographical sketches of various family members and other individuals mentioned in this book contain additional information about what happened to them during the war while I was imprisoned and events after the war.

Bernhard Liebster. From the time of "Crystal Night" until I found my dying father in Sachsenhausen concentration camp, I knew nothing about the fate of my family. But the Reichenbach archives contain correspondence between my sister Hanna, then in Argentina, and the Reichenbach city office. These documents mention the deportation of my family to the Polish border via Darmstadt. This was an effort to force my family to return to Poland. German officials designated my family as Polish, but the Polish authorities refused them entry. It is not clear when my family then returned to Reichenbach. The family had to pay 300 reichsmarks for their own deportation! During their absence, the windows of our little house were shattered and the place was looted. Also, Aunt Settchen Oppenheimer was taken to an old-age home. I discovered through our recent research that she became a victim of the Nazi "euthana-sia" program. It is not known why only my mother, Bertha (Babette), could escape to Argentina. In Reichenbach, I recently met an eye-witness who remembered that the Nazis forced my father, Bernhard, to run seven kilometers, totally naked, from Reichenbach to Bensheim. Together with other Jews, he was sent to prison and then camp. My father died in Sachsenhausen on April 9, 1940.

The Eckstein Family. When conditions became more dangerous for Jews, the Ecksteins moved to Pforzheim in the province of Baden Württemberg. Jews there were rounded up and sent to Gurs transit camp in southern France. The camp originally held Span-ish Republican prisoners from the Civil War, as well as French political prisoners. At least one Jehovah's Witness, an Armenian, was also held there. The officials of Baden Württemberg wanted to present Hitler with a "*judenrein*" land, that is, a land free of Jews, and the French offered Gurs as a holding place for Jews ousted from the region. The Ecksteins were on a transport to Gurs. Later, perhaps from 1943 onward, virtually all Jews in France were turned over to Nazi authorities. The Ecksteins, along with their son and daughter, were then taken from Gurs and sent to Theresienstadt, and it is there that they likely perished.

Julius, Hugo, and Leo Oppenheimer. Julius and Hugo managed to emigrate after "Crystal Night." The mobs had looted 130,00 reichsmarks worth of merchandise, after which the business was "Aryanized." The two brothers first stopped at Cuba and then went on to New York. Their brother, Leo, was forced to sell his candy business in Viernheim to an "Aryan." He then had to do forced labor in a factory in Mannheim. Leo had to move his family of seven into a small apartment there. On October 22, 1940, they were arrested. The local police and Nazi officials marched them through the city. The next morning, they boarded a transport to France. Passing from one French camp to another, they finally ended up in the transit camp of Gurs. One day in 1942, they overheard someone say that Mrs. Oppenheimer's name was on a list of prisoners to be deported to the east. Leo and his family decided to attempt an escape. They succeeded in crossing the Pyrenees Mountains to Spain and from there went to Portugal, where they obtained visas to enter the United States. Leo settled in California, where he opened a wholesale candy business.

Leopold Liebster. My father's brother, Leopold, hid in Stuttgart. Perhaps because his wife was Catholic and his neighbors did not turn him in to the Gestapo, he was able to remain hidden. After the war, Uncle Leopold was of great help to my mother, seeing that she received a small compensation payment for our lost property. Leopold's son, Alfred, emigrated to the United States, where he married. Alfred and his wife, Christa, often traveled between New York and Stuttgart to care for his parents until their deaths, living up to the meaning of our name Liebster ("beloved one"). Alfred and Christa have two sons; thus the Liebster name lives on.

Ruth Heinz. During a recent visit to Germany to participate in exhibition programs, my wife, Simone, and I met an older woman who introduced herself as Ruth. She was the German girl in Viernheim who had been brave enough to dance with a Jew! For her courage, she had endured insults and sharp criticism. I learned that her parents had been arrested for being Jehovah's Witnesses and were sent to a camp. Although her parents told her nothing about their secret religious activities, probably for her own safety, she had been taught from an early age that God is not partial. Soon after we met at the ball, however, Jews were totally barred from entering the dance hall.

Kindinger the Communist. The man who helped to save my life had been an active member of the Communist Party in Reichenbach. He was arrested during the early days of the Nazi regime. He was a stonemason, a member of a well-established family in Reichenbach, though I never met him until I encountered him in Buchenwald. Kindinger served in the camp as a *Blockältester* (block overseer) for many years and is remembered as a resister of the Nazi regime.

Friedrich ("Fritz") Heikorn. Born in 1915 in Olmutz, Czechoslovakia, Fritz faced antisemitic discrimination while attending *Realgymnasium* (the school for 12- to 19-year-old students). The Heikorn family owned a large factory and employed 600 workers who made condiments, soap, and kosher margarine. Through the rabbi Dr. Oppenheimer, Fritz received a thorough religious education. After graduation Fritz became an expert accountant for his father's firm. When Nazi forces occupied the Sudetenland in March 1939, they razed the synagogue that served 3,000 Jews in Böhmen and Mähren counties. On September 1, 1939, Fritz was arrested. He was first sent to Dachau and then to Buchenwald. His mother was put in Ravensbrück and Auschwitz. His younger sister Gertrude went to Theresienstadt and later to the Baltics, where she disappeared. His maternal aunt, grandparents, and uncles all perished in Auschwitz. Of Fritz's family, only his father escaped and emigrated. Fritz later graduated from the Watchtower Bible School of Gilead and went on to live a full and active life.

Hugo Holzmann. Hugo was the son of a Jewish father and a German mother who converted to Judaism. His father died while Hugo was a boy, and his mother adhered to her adopted faith despite the Nazi threat. Even though she was ethnically German, because she wore a yellow star, she received reduced food rations for Hugo and his sister. Hugo's mother was able to find places for her and the children with Bavarian farmers. The three had to stay on the move constantly. Those hiding them put themselves at tremendous risk.

Hugo's courageous mother managed to hide the family safely until the end of the war. I met Hugo on our journey across the Atlantic when his family was moving to the United States. I have kept in touch with him ever since. Simone and I had occasion to visit him in California. Just lately he wrote us that he is preparing for the Bar Mitzvah of his grandson.

Sydney Nussbaum. My brother-in-law Sydney lost his father and his four uncles in World War I. They fought on the German side. Sydney was left to be raised by the five widows, who lived close by. He worked as an electrician in Hamburg until his workplace was destroyed on "Crystal Night." At that time Sydney was taken to Buchenwald. But his immigration papers arrived in time to gain him release from the camp. He married my sister Ida before leaving for the United States so that he could bring her over once he arrived. Besides Sydney, only his brother Fred and his cousin's two daughters survived. The parents were given permission to send one of their two daughters to Palestine. On the day of the oldest daughter's departure, the family stood in tears at the railroad station. The girl had her permission ticket hung around her neck. As she boarded the train, another girl next to her panicked and jumped off the train. She quickly grabbed the girl's name tag and hung it around her sister's neck. Thus, both daughters escaped to Palestine. The girls suffered lifelong emotional trauma. Sydney, a hardworking man, tried to drown out the tragedies of the past by putting all of his energies into his thriving business.

Charles Eicher. Charlie was born into a Protestant family in Alsace-Lorraine, a region at that time controlled by Germany, though it had previously been under French rule. He came in contact with the *Bibelforscher* before the outbreak of World War I. His conscience moved him to refuse to comply when called up for the army. He hid in his sister's house in Mulhouse. She had a double floor in the attic where Charlie stayed, with only enough room to lie down or sit up. He remained there until Mulhouse was liberated from the Germans. After the war, he worked as an art designer before emigrating to the United States, where he applied his talents as an artist for the WatchTower Society. I will always remember the warmhearted welcome that Charlie gave to me and to other newcomers from Europe.

APPENDICES

A. *A Day in Buchenwald*

B. The Camps

C. Nazi Propaganda

- Law for the Safeguard of German Blood and of German Honor

- Cleaning Up Nazi Anti-Jewish Propaganda Prior to 1936 Olympics in Berlin, Germany

- SA Report Following the November 9/10, 1938, Pogrom

- The Aftermath of "Crystal Night"

- Viernheim Youth Marches

- The Day of Victory

- "They Will Never Be Free Again…" (Hitler Speech)

D. "A Witness Testimony" CETJAD Traveling Exhibition

Appendix A

A DAY IN BUCHENWALD

The sun is smiling
Above me the sky is bright
But inside, my heart is tight.

How cruelly misplaced
Bird song seems
Where thousands were killed.

This is a place silence demanding
Where every smile must freeze,
A place laughter forbidding.

How much torment endured,
How many lives lost?
So carelessly taken ...

What suffering inflicted
Such crimes committed
At one man's behest!

"To each his own"
sneers the gate above,
a mournful heart is mine.

The feelings that fill me
Are pity and rage,
Helpless anger burns.

How cold, how dull
The hearts of those
Who caused this agony.

A door falling shut
Resounds in these rooms,
An eerie gunshot ...

My God, how I thank Thee
That I freedom enjoy,
That you granted this gift.

Never was I forced to suffer
Am still able to laugh
Pain and sorrow pass by me.

And yet I am wistful,
These bloodstained roads
Hold me captive ...

Written by Alicia Karlstroem, age 16,
the day a memorial stone for
Jehovah's Witnesses was unveiled by
Max Liebster and Rikola-Gunnar Lüttgenau,
deputy director of the Buchenwald Memorial,
at Buchenwald concentration camp,
May 9, 2002.

"Man muß Gott mehr gehorchen als den Menschen"
Apostelgeschichte 5,29

In Erinnerung an Jehovas Zeugen die aus religiösen Gründen
verfolgt wurden und hier litten oder starben

"We must obey God rather than men"
Acts 5,29

In Remembrance of Jehovah's Witnesses Who Suffered and Died Here,
Persecuted Because of Their Religious Beliefs

Appendix B

THE CAMPS
(in chronological order according to Max Liebster's narrative)

Sachsenhausen. This large camp, located near Berlin, Germany, was erected by inmates and opened in 1936. In the original camp, more than 80 barracks formed a semicircle around the sprawling roll call grounds. In November 1938, nearly 2,000 Jews were sent to the camp. The inmate population was used for forced labor. Jews lived in especially brutal conditions. Many prisoners were tortured by being forced to perform calisthenics, such as the infamous "Saxon greeting," or Sachsengruss, until they dropped from exhaustion. In early 1945 the prisoner population reached nearly 48,000. About 18,000 prisoners were killed that year before the "death marches," or evacuation of the camp, began in April 1945.

Neuengamme. Situated on the Elbe River near Hamburg, Germany, this camp was set up in December 1938 as a subcamp of Sachsenhausen. It became an independent camp in the summer of 1940. The initial prisoner population was predominantly German. But later in the war, non-German prisoners, including captured Russian soldiers, filled the camp. Slave-labor projects included construction of the camp, a brick works, a munitions factory, a canal excavation, and clay mining. Working and "living" conditions were such that prisoners died by the hundreds. Neuengamme held more than 95,000 prisoners in its last five years of operation. About 56,000 inmates perished in Neuengamme. An additional 10,000 fell victim to brutal death marches from the camp in the last days of the war.

Auschwitz-Birkenau (Auschwitz II). The death factory Auschwitz, symbolic of the Nazi program of annihilation, consisted of three main camps. Construction of Auschwitz I began in May 1940, and it was the site of bizarre medical experiments on prisoners. Built beginning in October 1941, Auschwitz-Birkenau, or Auschwitz II, had the largest prisoner population and included sections for men and women, and a special section for Roma (Gypsies). The first gas chambers began operating in January 1942, but the largest gas chambers, which included crematorium ovens, were built in 1943. The SS poured one or two cans of Zyklon B pellets into the sealed gas chamber. When exposed to air, the bluish pellets, which were normally used for fumigation, released a highly lethal cyanide gas that could asphyxiate a person within minutes. The bodies were then taken to the crematorium ovens to be burned. At times, children were not gassed but were taken directly to the crematorium, where they were thrown into the ovens alive. Trains arrived daily with transports of Jews from across Europe. In excess of 6,000 were killed and burned daily. Nearly 440,000 Hungarian Jews went to their death in Auschwitz in 1944 between May and July. About 1.1 million Jews were murdered in Auschwitz-Birkenau, along with tens of thousands of Poles, Roma, and Soviet prisoners of war.

Auschwitz-Buna (Auschwitz III, or Monowitz). Dozens of German companies set up factories near Auschwitz in order to reap huge profits at the expense of slave laborers. I. G. Farben, one such company, is an industrial giant to this day. During the war, I. G. Farben supplied most of Germany's synthetic oils, gas, and rubber, along with explosives and poison gases. The I. G. Auschwitz plant was erected in 1943 and was at the time the largest producing plant in the world. About 25,000 inmates died in Buna, and the average life expectancy of a Jewish inmate was three to four months.

Buchenwald. The camp was established near Weimar, Germany, in July 1937. In the early days, the camp held German political prisoners, Jews, Jehovah's Witnesses, and homosexuals. But with the start of World War II, large numbers of non-German prisoners poured into the camp and its numerous subcamps. As Allied forces closed in on German lines in early 1945, prisoners from Auschwitz and Gross-Rosen were evacuated to Buchenwald. Just before American forces reached the camp, the SS evacuated 28,000 prisoners by foot and rail. But the attempt to empty the camp failed, and about 21,000 prisoners were liberated from Buchenwald on April 11, 1945. Of the estimated total camp population of 250,000, about 50,000 perished in Buchenwald.

Further Reading

Feig, K. G. (1979). *Hitler's Death Camps.* New York: Holmes & Meier Publishers, Inc.

Garbe, D. (1999). *Zwischen Widerstand und Martyrium—die Zeugen Jehovas im "Dritten Reich."* Munich: Oldenbourg.

Gilbert, M. (1988). *Atlas of the Holocaust.* New York: William Morrow and Company, Inc.

Hackett, D. A. (1995). *The Buchenwald Report.* Boulder, CO: Westview Press.

Hesse, H. (ed.) (2000). *Persecution and Resistance of Jehovah's Witnesses During the Nazi Regime—1933-1945.* Bremen, Germany: Edition Temmen.

Hilberg, R. (1967). *The Destruction of the European Jews.* Chicago: Quadrangle Books.

Taylor, J., & Shaw, W. (1987). *The Third Reich Almanac.* New York: World Almanac.

Appendix C

NAZI PROPAGANDA

LAW FOR THE SAFEGUARD OF GERMAN BLOOD
AND OF GERMAN HONOR

15 September 1935

Certain in the knowledge that the purity of the German blood is the fundamental necessity for the continuation of the German people, and endowed with an unflinching will to secure the German nation for all times to come, the Reichstag has unanimously approved the following law, which is herewith made public:

§ 1

Marriages between Jews and citizens of German or German-related blood are forbidden. Marriages which have been performed in spite of this law, even if they have been performed in a foreign country, are void.

Complaints declaring them void can originate only with the District Attorney.

§ 2

Extramarital sexual intercourse between Jews and citizens of German or German-related blood are forbidden.

§ 3

Jews are not allowed to employ female citizens of German or German-related blood under 45 years in their household.

§ 4

(1) Jews are forbidden to raise the Reich and National flag, and they cannot show the National colors.

(2) However, they are allowed to display the Jewish colors. The exercise of this disposition is under the state's protection.

§ 5

(1) Whoever acts against Paragraph 1 will be punished with forced labor.

(2) The man who acts against Paragraph 2 will be punished with prison or forced labor.

(3) Whoever acts against Paragraph 3 or 4 will be punished with prison not exceeding one year and with a fine, or with one of these punishments.

§ 6

The Secretary of the Interior will, together with the Deputy Führer and the Attorney General, issue the necessary law and administrative ordinances.

§ 7

This law is valid on the date of its publication, but Paragraph 3 will be valid only as of 1 January, 1936.

Nuremberg, 15 September 1935, National Party Liberty Congress

Der Führer and Reich Chancellor

(signed) Adolf Hitler

Cleaning Up Nazi Anti-Jewish Propaganda Prior to 1936 Olympics in Berlin, Germany

The Führer's Representative
Munich, January 29, 1936

    The Brown House

To the Gauleiter
Circulation Memo No. 18/36

Some of the signs and placards in which counties, municipalities and restaurants indicate that Jews are not welcome are made in bad taste.

When posting such signs, I kindly ask you to take into consideration that travelling foreigners in Germany observe carefully the measures we take against the Jews. In reality the majority of these strangers basically welcome the German measures against international Jewry. The German reputation in foreign countries will therefore not suffer because of our legislation regarding the Jews but will most likely if there are any distasteful or exaggerated individual representations or portrayals [against Jews].

I ask therefore to be careful that only signs and placards are posted that express without any specific spitefulness that Jews are not welcome. (For example, signs "Jews are not wanted here" or something similar.) I especially request to refrain from signs which indicate the possibility of punishment for the Jews, e.g., "Jews enter this location at their own risk," and similar threatening remarks.

                                        Signed by Rudolf Hess

SA Report Following the November 9/10, 1938, Pogrom

Darmstadt, November 11, 1938
Moosbergstreet 2
SA. Of the NSDAP
Brigade 50 (Starkenburg)

To
SA Unit Kurpfalz
Mannheim

On November 10, 1938, 3 pm, the following order reached me:

"On orders of the unit commander, all synagogues within the territory of brigade 50 are to be blown up or burned down immediately. Adjacent buildings housing Aryan occupants are not to be damaged. This operation is to be carried out in civilian clothes. Mutiny and looting are to be stopped. Report concerning execution of orders is to be submitted to the brigade leader or the office by 8:30."

The unit leaders were immediately alerted and meticulously instructed by me and they proceeded to execute the operation immediately.

I herewith report that the following destruction took place in
Unit 115

1.	Synagogue in Darmstadt, Bleichstrasse,		destroyed by fire		
2.	" " "	Fuchsstrasse	"	"	"
3.	" " "	O./Ramstadt	interior and furnishings smashed		
4.	" " "	Gräfenhausen	"	"	"
5.	" " "	Griesheim	"	"	"
6.	" " "	Pfungstadt	"	"	"
7.	" " "	Eberstadt	destroyed by fire		

...

The Aftermath of "Crystal Night"

Report about the Municipal Council Meeting dated November 11, 1938:

> ...At the end of the agenda was the defensive battle against the Jewry on 11/10 and its accompanying circumstances. It was understandable that the churned up [German] soul defended itself on the occasion of the Jewish boy's murder in Paris, and in justified anger retaliated to the Jews what their international *clique* did to the German hostland; but it is reprehensible that individuals tried to enrich themselves with the property of the [German] nation. Everything the Jews accumulated in Germany through swindle belongs to the German people... Therefore, it is urgently requested that the taken goods...be immediately returned to the Police. Violations to this notice will be prosecuted.

Viernheim's Youth Marches

On Saturday evening Hitler Youth, *Jungvolk* [Young People], BDM [League of German Girls] and BDJM [League of Young German Girls] paraded through the streets with their flags and unit pennants, singing as a music company and advertising their Hitler Youth magazine "Fanfare" to the upper Western region. At 7 p.m. all met for a rally in front of the Town Hall, where Youth leader Schmitt spoke informatively to the comrades about the "Goals of the Hitler Youth" and their battle magazine "Fanfare." "Hitler Youth stand for none other than service, and the slogan for youth is battle. Our claim to leadership of the youth is a title we have fought for ourselves, and we will pursue and carry out this claim unrelentingly until we have reached the goal of transforming the entire young generation in Germany according to Hitler Youth precepts. We transcend religious groupings and overcome the barricades of reactionism. We will turn Hitler's revolutionary Labor Youth into a Socialist German *Volk* (people). The Hitler Youth serves as an eternal fountain of youth for this movement. It will never run dry and always furnish National Socialism with new energy."

Concluding the rally, they sang their battle song "Our banner flutters before us."

The Day of Victory

This was the day, at last to bear weapons,
The day we struck the dragon,
Called cowardice and boyish mischief,
The day our Fatherland awoke.

That day has now become a year,
A year of battle, victory and labor,
It was the year of new German growth,
The year of storming and of deeds.

Who, though, crushed the strength of weeds,
Purged the seedlings and took the plow,
Whose vigilant effort was it day and night
To bravely, loyally watch the German field?

A shout of joy resounds across the field:
Hail you, my Führer, Germany's shelter and hero!
Continue on to sow; we are your seedlings!
Wherever you plant us, we'll ripen to deeds.

From blossom to blossom and fruit to fruit,
A noble plant in German honour grows,
A crop incomparable in glory and richness:
Germany's Third Reich!

"They will never be free again…"

"This youth learns nothing but to think German and to act German. When these boys enter our organization at the age of ten, it is often the first time in their lives that they get to breathe and feel fresh air; then four years later they come from the Jungvolk into the Hitler Youth, and we keep them there for another four years, and then we definitely don't put them back into the hands of the originators of our old classes and status barriers; rather we take them straight into the Party or into the Labor Front, the SA, or the SS, the NSKK [motorized corps] and so on. And if they are there for another two years or a year and a half and still haven't become complete National Socialists, then they go into the Labor Service and are polished for another six or seven months, all with a symbol, the German spade. And any class consciousness or pride of status that may be left here and there is taken over by the Wehrmacht for further treatment for two years, and when they come back after two, three, or four years, we take them straight into the SA, SS, and so on again, so that they shall in no case suffer a relapse, and they will never be free again as long as they live."

Adolf Hitler, December 2, 1938
Reichenbach

Appendix D

"A Witness Testimony" CETJAD Traveling Exhibition (Spanish edition)

Ejes ideológicos del nazismo

*   Omnipotencia y omnipresencia del Estado. Se subordina todo al Estado totalitario. Se suprime toda oposición política, intelectual, religiosa y social. El gobierno dictatorial nazi interviene en la economía y la regimentación social.

*   Protagonismo de la elite. Se parte de la idea de que no todos los hombres merecen los mismos derechos. Solo una clase elegida tiene la capacidad de gobernar y liderar a las masas. Se practica un darvinismo social que elimina a las razas consideradas inferiores, como los judíos o los gitanos. Se planea acabar con los enfermos y se limita el campo de acción de la mujer.

*   Imperialismo. Apelando a la necesidad de espacio vital, el nazismo se lanza a la conquista de nuevos territorios. El régimen de Hitler fomenta en sus súbditos un patriotismo y nacionalismo exacerbado, así como un desprecio absoluto a las poblaciones de los territorios que rodean Alemania.

*   Exaltación del jefe carismático. Se fomenta la devoción absoluta a la figura del Fürher. Todo súbdito alemán debe prestarle a Hitler obediencia ciega y seguirle sin titubeos.

*   Desconfianza en la razón. El nazismo rechaza de plano la tradición racionalista. Ninguna premisa nazi puede someterse a discusión. Se exaltan únicamente los elementos irracionales de la conducta, los sentimientos intensos, las emociones y el fanatismo.

11

Essentials of Nazi ideology

Articles and illustrations appearing in literature published by
Jehovah's Witnesses during the Nazi era

Profile of Auschwitz extermination camp

SACHSENHAUSEN

A partir de marzo de 1938, Sachsenhausen recibe a los *Bibelforscher*. Se les mantiene aislados y se les niegan los derechos otorgados a los demás detenidos. Ni periódicos, ni libros, y sobre todo nada de correspondencia. Más tarde, se les permitirá una carta de cinco renglones por mes. Una instrucción de las SS decía de ellos: «Hay que ganárselos mediante la adulación, puesto que el rigor ejercido contra ellos tiene por efecto fortalecer su determinación».

Esta traducción alemana de la Biblia pertenecía a Johann Stossier. Poco después de su ejecución, las tropas aliadas la encontraron sobre su cuerpo.

▼ Johann Stossier: Austria

Nació el 29 de mayo de 1909 en Techelsberg. Ejecutado.

Formaba parte de una compañía de teatro y se hizo Testigo de Jehová poco antes de 1930. Fue detenido en abril de 1940 y deportado a Neuengamme y, más tarde, a Sachsenhausen. Aunque el reglamento interior del campo lo prohibía, consiguió hacerse con una pequeña Biblia. Fue ejecutado poco antes de la liberación.

La ejecución de August Dickmann

August Dickmann fue arrestado por la Gestapo. Después de ser juzgado y cumplir su sentencia, firmó la «declaración» de renuncia a su fe. Pese a ello, en octubre de 1937 fue enviado al campo de Sachsenhausen. Allí pidió que se anulara la declaración que había firmado. Al estallar la Segunda Guerra Mundial comenzaron a enviarse cartas de reclutamiento militar. A August Dickmann le enviaron la suya a su domicilio tres días después de comenzar la guerra y su esposa se la envió al campo. Allí, ante los mismos oficiales del campo, rehusó firmar su hoja de reclutamiento. El comandante del campo, un tal Baranowsky, apodado «Cuadrangular», informó de ello a Himmler y solicitó la ejecución pública de Dickmann. Himmler respondió que Dickmann estaba condenado a muerte y debía ser ejecutado.

Era viernes. Un profundo silencio cubrió el campo cuando un pelotón vino a preparar el patio para la ejecución. Circulaban todo tipo de rumores. La tensión se apoderó de los detenidos cuando se les informó que tendrían que dejar de trabajar una hora antes de lo acostumbrado. Todos los detenidos recibieron la orden de salir al patio. A los más de trescientos Testigos de Jehová, entre los cuales estaba el hermano de August Dickmann, Heinrich, se les colocó detrás del pelotón de ejecución. La voz de «Cuadrangular» se escuchó por los altavoces: «August Dickmann, nacido el 7 de enero de 1910, se niega a prestar servicio militar. Ha dicho: "El que derrame sangre humana verá su sangre derramada". Se ha colocado fuera de la sociedad y según las órdenes del jefe de las SS, Himmler, ha de ser ejecutado».

August Dickmann fue asesinado de tres disparos en la espalda.

Gerrit Benink en 1993, con su fiambrera de Sachsenhausen.

▼ Gerrit Benink: Países Bajos

Detenido el 18 de marzo de 1941.
Cárceles: Eindhoven y Herfogenbosch.
Campos: Sachsenhausen, Düsseldorf, Alderney, Buchenwald, Neuengamme.
Liberado el 5 de mayo de 1945.

Campo de concentración de Sachsenhausen

A: Barracones de las SS.
B: Plaza de revista.
C: Celdas.
D: Celdas de aislamiento.
E: Local de espulgamiento.
F: Lugar de ejecución.
G: Cámara de gas.

52

Jehovah's Witnesses in Sachsenhausen concentration camp

Jehovah's Witnesses in Buchenwald concentration camp

Index